John Fawssett visited his first Greek Islands soon after the end of the Second World War, as a very junior naval officer, when his ship was part of a squadron engaged in clearing live mines from Greek waters.

Subsequent commissions in other warships on station in the Mediterranean led to visits to many parts of Greece, including a three-day walking expedition among the monasteries of the Mount Athos peninsula.

During a second career in fruit growing he was able, with his wife, to take regular mid-winter motorcaravanning holidays in various parts of the Mediterranean. They have recently returned to their home in Sussex after living abroad for three years in their motor caravan.

Dedication

To my dearest Hannelore.
'And all things flourish where you turn your eyes'
(From Pastorals, by Alexander Pope)

Acknowledgements

A writer of travel guides can hardly be expected to be expert in the interpretation of ancient history. For a general view I am happy to rely on the writings of Professor A.R. Burn in, amongst others, *The Pelican History of Greece.*

My very grateful thanks to the National Tourist Organisation of Greece for their assistance in London, Argostoli and, especially, Patras.

The author and publisher would like to thank the following for their generous permission to use certain photographs:
Mr Nikos Katopodis for the two colour photos of Levkas.
Miss Vassiliki Bali for the two colour photos of Kefallonia.
Viamare Travel of 33 Mapesbury Road, London NW2 4HT for the pictures of Adriatic car ferries *Ionian Galaxy* (Strinzis Lines) and *Ouranos* (Fragline).

All other photos were taken by the author.

Front Cover: Fisherman with nets on the waterfront at Sami (Kefallonia).

Greek Island Series
Kefallonia
and the South Ionian Islands

John Fawssett

Ithaka · Levkas · Zakynthos

Roger Lascelles, Cartographic and Travel Publisher
47 York Road, Brentford, Middlesex TW8 0QP   Telephone: 01-847 0935

Publication Data

Title	Kefallonia and the South Ionian Islands
Typeface	Phototypeset in Compugraphic Times
Photographs	John Fawssett (unless otherwise indicated)
Index	Jane Thomas
Printing	Kelso Graphics, Kelso, Scotland.
ISBN	0 903909 76 6
Edition	This first, Jul 1989
Publisher	Roger Lascelles
	47 York Road, Brentford, Middlesex, TW8 0QP.
Copyright	John Fawssett

Distribution

Africa:	South Africa —	Faradawn, Box 17161, Hillbrow 2038
Americas:	Canada —	International Travel Maps & Books, P.O. Box 2290, Vancouver BC V6B 3W5
	U.S.A. —	Boerum Hill Books, P.O. Box 286, Times Plaza Station, Brooklyn, NY 1121T, (718-624 4000)
Asia:	India —	English Book Store, 17-L Connaught Circus/P.O. Box 328, New Delhi 110 001
	Singapore —	Graham Brash Pte Ltd., 36-C Prinsep St.
Australasia	Australia —	Rex Publications, 413 Pacific Highway, Artarmon NSW 2064. 428 3566
Europe:	Belgium —	Brussels - Peuples et Continents
	Germany —	Available through major booksellers with good foreign travel sections
	GB/Ireland —	Available through all booksellers with good foreign travel sections.
	Italy —	Libreria dell'Automobile, Milano
	Netherlands —	Nilsson & Lamm BV, Weesp
	Denmark —	Copenhagen - Arnold Busck, G.E.C. Gad, Boghallen, G.E.C. Gad
	Finland —	Helsinki — Akateeminen Kirjakauppa
	Norway —	Oslo - Arne Gimnes/J.G. Tanum
	Sweden —	Stockholm/Esselte, Akademi Bokhandel, Fritzes, Hedengrens. Gothenburg/Gumperts, Esselte. Lund/Gleerupska
	Switzerland —	Basel/Bider: Berne/Atlas; Geneve/Artou; Lausanne/Artou: Zurich/Travel Bookshop

Contents

Part 1: Planning Your Holiday

Part 2: The South Ionian Islands

Part 3: Mainland excursions

Appendices

Index

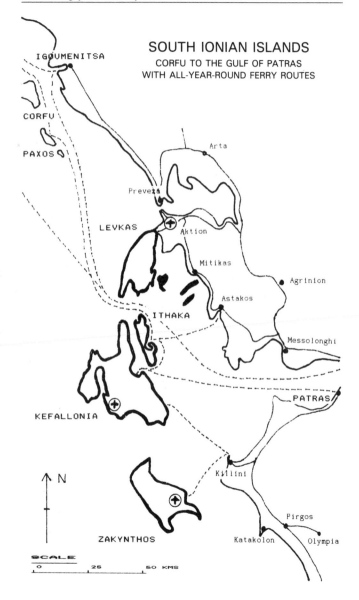

SOUTH IONIAN ISLANDS
CORFU TO THE GULF OF PATRAS
WITH ALL-YEAR-ROUND FERRY ROUTES

ONE

Why the South Ionian Islands?

It's a thought that I've often had before, and I dare say that you have too; but that day it struck me more forcibly than ever before. As it happens I was on my way to Greece, driving down through Italy to catch the ferry. I'd made an early start that morning, and as I approached Rome a pallid blood-red ball of sun was toiling to lift itself through the filthy pall of smoke overhanging the 'Eternal City'. Minutes later I was hurtling round the Gran Raccordo Annulare, dicing with death as speed-crazed Jehus overtook me right and left. My own sense of relief to have emerged unscathed into the Autostrada del Sole was tempered by the solid phalanxes of stationary vehicles choking the other carriageway, enveloped in their exhaust fumes, the pale faces of fretting drivers rigid with tension. Soon the advance of my own stream of traffic slumped to crawling pace and a single lane at the onset of roadworks. I passed regiments of bowing and scraping mechanical diggers, gouging out and stripping the embankments, part of some urgent work-programme to add yet another scar to the tarmac jungle. And then it was that the last straw materialised, kilometre upon kilometre of uprooted bushes of pink and white oleanders strewn beside the concrete's edge, wantonly ripped from the central reservation, poor cast-off wreaths in memoriam to the values of a passing civilisation — 'butchered to make a Roman motorway'!

Surely Man was not made to live like this! And even if he must, is not the pace of change and the degradation of our environment too rapid for most of us to adapt to, with so few generations to span the days since the passing of the horse and cart? Stop the world! I want to get off — so we may wish, but cannot! Then at least let there be left some oases of tranquillity, springs of refreshment, where we can withdraw from time to time to retune our bodies and recharge the cosmic batteries of the soul!

The next morning I watched a brilliant sun soaring through pure air over a transparent and unpolluted Ionian sea. Our ferry powered smoothly southwards, past gliding yachts and caiques hauling their nets. Later I sat on a coiled hawser in the bows, munching a crust of bread and quaffing an honest wine, as I gazed to port at the white cliffs of Levkas and Sappho's Leap, and the Ithaka of Odysseus to starboard, merging mistily into the mountains of Kefallonia. That evening I stood once more on Greek soil; I could have kissed it!

The South Ionian Islands

The euphony in the names Ionian and Aegean seems to encapsulate much of the difference of character between them. Both of course are Greek, but the Ionian is more feminine. Its air seems softer, its winds gentler, the clarity of its light less blindingly intense, its landscapes greener and more fertile. Happy we, who can choose to enjoy one of them, or the other, or even both!

Ionian islands is a convenient label, whose actual significance is open to debate. The most common definition derives from the Eptanisos of colonial times, whose seven principal members were Corfu, Paxos, Levkas, Kefallonia, Ithaka, Zakynthos and Kythira. Corfu and Paxos are clearly situated in the north part of the Ionian — that sea area south of the heel of Italy, bounded to the east by the west coasts of Greece and its Peloponnese (and soon to be covered in a further guidebook *Corfu and the North Ionian Islands*). **Kefallonia, Ithaka** and **Zakynthos,** major islands lying in the western approaches to the Gulf of Patras, plainly qualify as Ionian islands and are the main subjects of this book. A few kilometres to the north of Kefallonia and Ithaka is **Levkas,** technically an island by virtue of the man-made canal which for more than two millenia has separated it from the mainland, and so legitimately this book's fourth main subject. The status of Kythira has always been anomalous, its situation close to the most easterly prong of the Peloponnese, on the margin between the two seas, no more appropriate for classification as Aegean than Ionian. Historically its linkage with the Ionian islands was little more than a convenience of conquest; today for practical purposes these weak links have almost withered away. Kythira is now administered from Piraeus, and it has transport links only with the eastern Peloponnese, Piraeus, Athens, Crete and the islands of the Saronic Gulf. These latter are considerably nearer than the Ionian islands; clearly they are more easily accessible; and so for these reasons

Kythira is included in the guidebook *Saronic Gulf Islands and Kythira* already published.

A number of minor islands have also been described here, among them **Meganisi, Kalamos, Kastos** and the **Strophades,** which have been grouped with the major island from which they are administered.

In addition to their own very considerable attractions, as a unit the South Ionian islands enjoy the great benefit of excellent transport links with north west Europe, both direct by air, and by sea via Italy. It is fortunate that this has not yet ruined any of them by excessive exposure to mass tourism, as might well be alleged in the case of Corfu.

Kefallonia

It's the largest island in the Ionian, dominated by its huge central mountain. Tourism is not a major industry, being confined to an up-market beach resort near the capital and a few small pockets elsewhere. The island has excellent beaches, dramatic and beautiful scenery, contrasting villages and a number of interesting natural curiosities, but to cover it extensively requires much time and effort as well as (preferably) your own private transport. Day trips to the other three islands and to the mainland are practicable.

Ithaka

A much smaller and more intimate island than Kefallonia, Ithaka is less sophisticated, and somewhat in the shadow of its giant neighbour. Plenty of adequate beaches, varied scenery and some glorious views make it quite appropriate for a simple family holiday. Yachtsmen can enjoy its secure harbours and the ample opportunity for safe sailing in sheltered waters close by. Day trips to Kefallonia, Levkas and the mainland are practicable. To get the best out of the island itself some understanding of its historic associations, and a feeling for the Homeric legend of the Odyssey, is needful. It is not for nothing that Ithaka can, in a literary sense, lay claim to be the most famous island in the world!

Levkas

Levkas is odd one out among our four main islands because of its extreme proximity to the mainland, which has subjected it to a different sequence of historical influences, the effects of which are evident even today. Overlooked by tourism until quite recently, its indefinable and unusual charm remains unspoiled, and much appreciated by holiday-makers looking for something different. Its size is just right, being neither too large nor small for active exploration during the holiday; whilst the pastoral delights of its varied landscape are mirrored in the friendly contentment of its people. Day trips to Ithaka, Kefallonia, its own offshore islands and a wide area of the mainland are practicable. It has excellent beaches, and is ideal for wind-surfing at all levels of expertise.

Zakynthos

The most complete holiday island of the group, Zakynthos has a well-developed array of tourist attractions to suit all tastes, based on a town and four beach resorts of contrasting character. Fine beaches with a very good range of watersports, varied and attractive scenery, some splendid church architecture, and organised excursions outside the island to Kefallonia and the mainland of the Peloponnese should make it first choice for many, among them all those who have not before experienced the Ionian islands.

Making comparisons

At this stage, some comparisons can usefully be made regarding aspects of particular concern to tourists.

- **Sophistication** Kefallonia and Zakynthos are the most sophisticated islands; Ithaka and Levkas the simplest.
- **Activities** Zakynthos and Kefallonia offer the greatest choice of things to do; Ithaka the least, with Levkas somewhere between.
- **Accommodation** Kefallonia and Zakynthos have the widest range of hotels, whilst villas and private rooms are widely available on all the islands. Because of its small size and few hotels, Ithaka might be the most difficult for finding accommodation at short notice.
- **Beaches** Kefallonia, Zakynthos and Levkas all have a number of excellent beaches; so much so that it's hard to judge which of them has the best beach or the highest general standard. The beaches of Ithaka are perfectly adequate.
- **Tourism** In relation to area and local population numbers Zakynthos is the most heavily committed to tourism, Ithaka the least. Kefallonia and Levkas fall between the other two.
- **Motor vehicles** All the islands have well-developed road networks, which enable all parts to be reached without difficulty.

Some roads in Zakynthos and Kefallonia suffer from rather frequent pot-holes. All islands have good car ferry services to the mainland and between one another.

● **Camping** Levkas is the island with most facilities for camping, closely followed by Zakynthos. Kefallonia has two good campsites, rather a small number for such a large island. Ithaka has no campsites, and few water supplies or other facilities specifically for campers.

The facts underlining these value judgements are elaborated in Part 2 of this volume.

Official information

NTOG The National Tourist Organisation of Greece is known inside Greece as EOT (pronounced like yacht). Its offices answer tourist queries, and hand out a number of free leaflets in several languages. Most of these cover specific areas, whereas the one entitled General Information about Greece contains a mass of detail useful for planning, which is updated annually. During summer a monthly list of ferries sailing from Piraeus and some other ports is distributed. The staff are mostly very helpful. NTOG offices relevant to this volume are at: London (195/197 Regent Street W1R 8DR0); Athens (inside the National Bank of Greece, 1 Karageorgi Servias Street — on a corner of Syntagma; also a second office inside the General Bank, on the corner of Syntagma/Ermon; Athens Airport (East); Piraeus; Patras; Igoumenitsa; Evzoni and Niki (road frontiers); and Argostoli (Kefallonia). There are also locally funded tourist information offices in Zakynthos, Ithaka and (due to open in 1989) Levkas.

Place Names The English spelling of Greek place names is a notorious pitfall, since various alternatives in regular use often exist. The versions preferred by NTOG are used whenever possible throughout this book, whilst the more common alternatives are mentioned where appropriate in Part 2. The sharp-eyed reader may notice a few discrepancies, when different versions sometimes appear even within the same paragraph. This was necessary because certain commercial organisations have chosen a contrary anglicised spelling for their name or product.

There does in fact exist an Hellenic Standard (ELOT 743) for the transliteration of Greek place names into English. But old habits die hard. For example, in one document professing to observe the standard, the same place name is variously spelt PEIRAIAS (new standard spelling) and PIRAEUS (traditional)!

Publications Two useful publications, written in English and published monthly, are widely available in Greece. Between them they contain the best available up-to-date travel information — indeed the NTOG monthly shipping sheet derives from one of them. Even so, it cannot be claimed that either is totally comprehensive, particularly for services originating in the provinces and islands. Your friendly Greek travel agent might be persuaded to give you one of his discarded copies.

— *Greek Travel Pages.* Price 1000drs. UK representative Timsway Holidays, Nightingales Corner, Little Chalfont, Bucks HP7 9QS.

— *Key Travel Guide.* Price 450drs. UK representative BAS Overseas Publications Ltd, 48-50 Sheen Lane, London SW14 8LP.

Tourist police These police officers are specially selected and trained to deal with tourist problems, to distribute tourist leaflets in places without a NTOG office, and to collect tourist statistics. They are more likely than other police to have some understanding of foreign languages. Until recently they were located in special tourist police stations, but following reorganisation are now usually found in small sections inside the regular police stations. In most parts of Greece they can be contacted directly on the telephone by dialling 171.

British Consul There is an honorary British Vice-consul in Patras at 2 Votsi Street, which is just off Othonas Amalias near the south entrance to the port. This charming lady will certainly do her best to help with major problems such as loss of passport, serious accident, death, or arrest. But there are so many tourists these days, too many of them expecting to get help which a consul is not permitted to give. The most common problems — several of them discussed later in this book — are:

- Charter flights. Don't come without a valid accommodation voucher.
- Moped hire (fully covered in Chapter 9).
- Drugs and contraband. Don't!
- Money. Bring enough! (The consul can make a loan only under exceptional circumstances.)
- Jobs. Opportunities are very limited because of local unemployment; moreover a working knowledge of Greek is usually essential.

Visas

For those holding a British or Irish passport the entry stamp entitles you to stay for six months. Renewal is a complicated procedure that involves getting a form from a notary, completing it (it is printed in Greek only), buying stamps from another office, providing five passport photographs, evidence that you have changed money and have means of support for the next three months and generally satisfying the police that you are not working. The length of the extended stay is at the discretion of the police.

A woman of Levkas in traditional (widow's) costume. Despite recent material progress her pastoral routine must be little different from that of her remote ancestors.

TWO

When to go

The **climate** of the Greek islands is very well suited to summer holidaymakers. Between April and September the sun shines almost all the time. May, September and October are probably the most favourable months, when temperatures are certain to be warm, but should not be too hot. July and August are the hottest months — although a lot less hot than on the mainland because of the cooling effects of wind and sea. The above is as true of the Ionian as the Aegean; what is more difficult is to pin down with statistics the difference between the climates of the two seas, though it seems evident when you encounter it.

Temperature tables are of little help for this. The figures for Kefallonia and Zakynthos in Table 1 show as much difference one from the other as with Aegean islands of comparable latitude. It will be noted that Zakynthos has fewer extremes of temperature and a slightly higher average than Kefallonia. Ithaka and Levkas have more in common with the latter.

Neither are **winds** so very different in the Ionian, responsive as they are to the same major pressure systems. In summer, for example, the Azores high and the Asian monsoon low (a depression in the general area of Pakistan) generate northerly winds in both Aegean and Ionian. But whereas the Aegean *meltemi* generally comes from the north east, in the Ionian its direction is nearer north west, and it's less strong. It usually begins around noon, to blow with a force between 2 and 5 before dying away at sunset. From time to time a stronger version known as the *maistro* comes from the north north west. More occasionally there is a southerly wind known as the *sirocco* which brings a period of sticky heat with it, sometimes carrying sand particles from the Sahara desert. Between October and the end of March winds tend to be from the south east — most gales are from that direction. Winter depressions can develop and move rapidly, but sometimes linger for long periods in the south of the Ionian. It is worth remembering that the ancient

Month	Kefallonia (Argostoli)			Zakynthos (Town)		
	min °C	av. °C	max °C	min °C	av. °C	max °C
Jan	6.6	11.0	14.4	8.7	11.4	14.4
Feb	7.6	11.3	14.6	8.2	11.5	13.3
Mar	9.0	13.0	17.5	10.0	13.2	15.8
Apr	11.11	5.8	21.0	12.1	16.0	18.9
May	14.3	19.6	24.5	15.6	19.8	23.2
Jun	17.7	23.7	28.9	20.0	24.0	27.9
Jul	19.8	26.3	31.2	22.1	27.8	29.9
Aug	20.1	28.4	32.1	22.2	27.1	30.0
Sep	18.8	23.8	30.0	20.1	24.2	27.8
Oct	15.7	19.8	24.7	16.6	20.2	23.2
Nov	12.2	15.8	21.6	13.2	16.5	18.8
Dec	8.9	12.7	16.6	10.1	13.1	15.8

Table 1: Average maximum, minimum and average monthly temperatures

Month	Av. no. of days with measurable rainfall			Av. amount of rainfall in mm.		
	KEF	ZAK	MYK	KEF	ZAK	MYK
Jan	13	14	13	126	187	82
Feb	12	13	11	104	142	59
Mar	9	11	8	83	93	38
Apr	7	8	5	54	53	20
May	4	6	5	25	27	16
Jun	3	4	2	18	15	3
Jul	1	1	0	5	2	0
Aug	1	2	1	11	13	1
Sep	3	5	1	30	37	7
Oct	10	11	6	136	144	27
Nov	12	14	9	138	211	55
Dec	15	18	13	170	228	81

Table 2: Average rainfall for Kefallonia (KEF), Zakynthos (ZAK) and Aegean Mykonos (MYK)

The gently sloping beach at Ag. Nikitas provides a safe playground for children.

Greeks used to suspend all their deep water shipping during the six months of winter, because of the danger from sudden and very fierce storms during that period.

There is a much more marked difference between amounts of **rainfall,** and Table 2 shows that Zakynthos enjoys nearly four times as much rainfall as Mykonos. Even more significant is that the period without useful amounts of rain continues in Mykonos for eight consecutive months, compared with only five in the Ionian; it is for this reason that the Ionian islands remain green and fertile throughout the year. Nor should the holidaymaker be over-concerned about summer rain, even in the Ionian, since usually it comes as a thunderstorm which passes within a couple of hours, and afterwards leaves the air feeling fresher. Humidity levels, though usually modest, are rather higher in the Ionian, and visibility distances less spectacular. The weather between November and March may be rather wet and cold, but there are not many tourists around then to share it with the islanders.

Table 3 shows that **seawater temperatures** at Zakynthos are warmer all the year than at Kefallonia. This is as one would expect, but the surprisingly large difference probably reflects some other factor, such as the situation of the recording stations.

Most people should find that the sea is quite warm enough for swimming during at least eight months of the year. However the transition from tepid bathwater to a tingling briskness may take place quite suddenly and unpredictably, when a late summer storm stirs up the sea to its very depths. But further cooling comes quite slowly, and keen swimmers will often find temperatures quite satisfactory even at Christmas time; indeed the water reaches its coldest around the beginning of March.

The rise and fall of **sea level** rarely exceeds three quarters of a metre, even at the time of spring tides.

	Jan	Feb	Mar	Apr	May	Jun
Kefallonia	12.5°C	12.6°C	12.5°C	14.1°C	17.6°C	20.6°C
Zakynthos	15.5°C	15.1°C	14.4°C	15.6°C	18.9°C	21.4°C
	Jul	Aug	Sep	Oct	Nov	Dec
Kefallonia	23.4°C	23.7°C	24.1°C	20.9°C	16.7°C	14.4°C
Zakynthos	23.8°C	24.3°C	22.7°C	22.5°C	18.5°C	17.0°C

Table 3: Seawater temperatures at sea surface

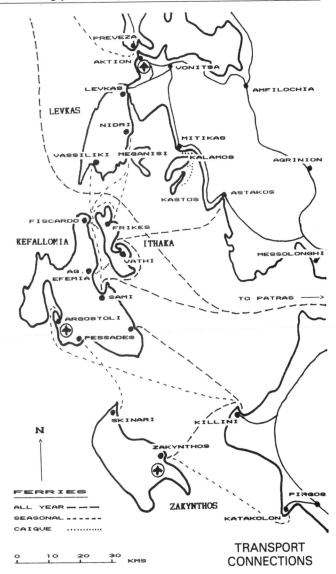

TRANSPORT
CONNECTIONS

THREE

Getting there

No other group of Greek islands offers so many and diverse ways of getting there as the Ionian islands. So many factors are involved — where you are starting from, what combination of islands you want to visit, the amount of time at your disposal, the season of the year and the depth of your pocket among others. It is possible to travel direct to Kefallonia, Zakynthos and Preveza (for Levkas) by charter flight, and motorists can drive direct to Levkas, thanks to the pontoon bridge which spans the channel separating it from the mainland. But for many visitors to these three islands and all visitors to Ithaka, which has no airport, the journey has to be done in stages in which ferries play an important role. This chapter, then, is inevitably complex and detailed, containing as it does information about all forms of international transport arriving directly in the islands themselves, and at those ports and airports bordering the Ionian Sea which link with the islands. It also lists the routes available for travel between the islands — further information will be found within the individual island chapters of Part 2. The question of getting to the islands via Athens — which may well be an effective and economical alternative — will be considered in the next chapter.

Departure points from mainland Greece to S. Ionian Islands

Preveza	— Levkas — Kefallonia, Ithaka)
Astakos	— Ithaka, Kefallonia
Patras	— Ithaka, Kefallonia
Killini	— Kefallonia, Zakynthos
Katakolon	— Zakynthos

The information given here dates from 1988, and includes some projections for 1989. Inevitably further changes will take place, though more likely they will come as further improvements. Most of the international services are quite well publicised, and should be known to competent travel agents. With some of the internal services it is otherwise; but you can be confident in advance that some practical connection between adjoining islands will exist throughout most of the year; for precise details you may well have to wait until your arrival in the area.

By air

Kefallonia and Zakynthos have their own airports; Levkas and Ithaka do not. But Levkas is well placed to take advantage of a nearby airport known as Preveza (Aktion), from which it can actually be quicker to get to Levkas than Preveza town. Ithaka is close enough to Kefallonia, with sufficiently frequent and reliable links by bus and ferry, to be able to make use of its airport. In summer too it is quite practicable to get to Ithaka from Preveza (Aktion) — for anyone prepared to get to grips with the complexity of the connection (see Chapter 12).

Scheduled There are no international flights direct to any of these three airports (but details of connections through Athens are given in the next chapter). It is possible to fly to Corfu, which has regular weekly services from London, Amsterdam, Geneva, Milan, Dusseldorf, Rome, Stockholm and Frankfurt. Onward travel would probably have to be by ferry, unless the timing of one of the occasional flights to Zakynthos, Kefallonia or Preveza was suitable.

Charter Direct charter flights from the UK to all three airports are available. The majority of seats will have been block-booked by tour operators, who sell most of them to their own clients as part of a packaged deal. Nevertheless flight-only seats often become available, and in the UK these are found advertised in the Sunday papers and magazines such as *Time Out* (see Part 2 for a list of regional UK airports for each island). International regulations require these seats to be sold in conjunction with an accommodation voucher, and your flight details will contain an address where the voucher may be accepted. But as this is normally provided at nominal cost (eg £2), it has to be understood that you are not expected to use it indeed you might find little more than a derelict building should you try to do so.

Seat-only passengers will probably not be covered by the tour operator's insurance for travel on his coaches from the airport, and so will be unable legally to make use of them. But taxis or public buses should be available at reasonable cost.

Charter flights, weekly

	1988	1989
Zakynthos	50	65 projected
Kefallonia	18	20 projected
Preveza (Aktion)	14	some increase

(more than half these flights originate in the UK)

By ship

The great majority of those travelling independently to the Ionian islands will choose one of the many vehicle ferries which shuttle across the Adriatic between Italy and Greece. Their routes fall into two groups:

● Long haul: starting from **Ancona, Venice** and **Trieste.** Long haul offers a less stressful journey, in larger and mostly more modern ships.

● Short haul: using ports down towards the 'heel' of Italy — **Brindisi, Bari** and **Otranto,** all in Apulia. Short haul can give a quicker overall journey; half as much time is spent confined on board ship; and the total cost of the journey will probably be less, though in either case fares are extremely reasonable by Western European standards.

Choice between long and short haul is a matter of personal preference. Details of the long and short haul routes are as follows:

From Ancona

Unless you have good reason to choose Venice or Trieste, Ancona with its easy road connections and shorter voyage is the port to head for. The majority of sailings depart in the evening, the remainder around midday. Competition between the four companies using the port ensures that you get good value for your money, but remember that high season rates apply generally during the whole of July and August, as well as September for the return to Italy — compared with a much briefer short haul peak (see below).

● Kareogeorgis: All year round twice weekly services (four times weekly July to October) direct to **Patras,** duration 32 hours. Two very large, relatively slow ships with swimming pool, *Mediterranean Sea* and *Mediterranean Sky* (both 16,000 tons). No discounts. UK agent: M.A.K. Travel and Tourism, 36 King Street, London WC2E 8JS.

● Strinzis: All year round twice weekly services (rising to daily during the summer peak) to **Patras** with calls at Corfu and Igoumenitsa. Stopover at Corfu permitted. Duration 34 hours. Three medium to fairly large fast ships with swimming pool, *Ionian Galaxy, Ionian Sun, Ionian Star* (4-10,000 tons). No discounts. During the peak season a subsidiary service is run to Patras via Yugoslavia (Split or Dubrovkik), duration 32 hours, stopover possible. UK agent: Viamare Travel, 33 Mapesbury Road, London NW2 4HT.

● Marlines: Twice weekly services (rising to daily during the summer peak) between March and December to **Patras** via Igoumenitsa, duration 32-34 hours. A mixed bag of three ships, ranging from the vast and fast *Queen M* (22,000 tons), through the very large *Countess M* (15,000 tons, swimming pool), to the fairly large *Princess* M (7,000 tons). Five per cent reduction on round trip fares. During the summer peak there is a weekly extension from Patras to Kusadasi or Izmir (Turkey) via Heraklion (Crete). UK agent: Viamare Travel, address as above.

● Minoan: This company specialised in the Piraeus-Crete route for many years, but has now deployed its largest and fastest ships between Ancona and **Patras,** with calls at Corfu and Igoumenitsa. Stopover at Corfu permitted. Duration 30-34 hours. Virtually an all-year-round service, with 2-5 services weekly. Very large fast ships with swimming pools, *El Greco, Fedra, King Minos* (all 19,000 tons). No discounts. U.K. Agent: P & O European Ferries, Channel House, Channel View Road, Dover, Kent CT17 9TJ.

From Trieste

● Hellenic Cypriot Mediterranean Lines. This company cut its teeth on developing a route between Volos and Tartous (Syria), calling at Rhodes and Limassol (Cyprus), which it continues to operate. It has recently deployed two medium sized ships *(Europa, Europa 2)* between Trieste and **Patras,** calling at Brindisi. Duration 42 hours. Discounts for children and students, and 20 per cent on the return fare for cars.

From Venice

● British Ferries Orient Express run their luxurious ferry *Orient Express* (12,500 tons) on the circular route Venice-Piraeus-Istanbul-Kusadasi-Patmos-**Katakolon**-Venice weekly, between March and November. The main objective is to provide high quality Eastern Mediterranean cruises, and prices are appropriate to that aim; but

Ionian Galaxy *(Strinzis Lines) employed on the long haul route between Ancona and Patras. Its particulars include: 9,898 GRT; max. speed 21 kts; 1,500 pax, 600 cars; casino, swimming pool, restaurants and shops.*

one-way and round-trip tickets to Greece are available for passengers and their vehicles (Katakolon is quite convenient for Zakynthos and Kefallonia, see below). Duration (Katakolon-Venice) 41/42 hours. UK agent: Sealink UK Ltd, Victoria Station, P O Box 29, London SW1V 1JX.

Ferries between Italy and Greece

	Departure points	Destinations	Ports of call
Long Haul	Ancona	Patras	Corfu
	Venice	Katakolon*	Igoumenitsa
	Trieste	(*see below)	Brindisi
Short Haul	Brindisi	Patras	Corfu
	Bari	Igoumenitsa	Kefallonia
	Otranto	Preveza	(connecting to Zakynthos/Levkas)
			Igoumenitsa
			Paxos
			Ithaka

Ships on the short haul routes are smaller, and tend to be older than those on the long haul. Virtually all sailings take place during a short period in the evening: the resulting competition between ferries to enter harbour ahead of their rivals often compels them to operate to the utmost limits of their engine capability, so generating considerably more vibration than the long haul ships, even though actual speeds are mostly slower. High season rates are generally limited to a couple of weeks around the beginning of August (but two weeks later for the return to Italy). Onward connections to Athens and Rome are available by coach or train.

From Brindisi

All but two of the companies operate from here, which historically was the main terminal for the rail ferry. Today so many ships use the port that at times its facilities can scarcely cope. Peculiar to Brindisi is an archaic requirement to take your boarding pass (issued by your ticket office) up to the second floor of the port office to get it stamped by the police — the equivalent procedures at Bari and Otranto are much more convenient. Nevertheless competition does ensure that all lines offer generous discounts — for example for children, students, motoring club members and European railcard holders, and on the return leg of round-trip tickets for both passengers and vehicles. But be suspicious of tickets which seem to give exceptional discounts, with which a few unscrupulous agents may entice you. There's a good chance that you'll be required to pay a surcharge as you board the ferry — an embarrassment that should not happen if you buy from the company's principal agent (who in any case is in a position to give you the best genuine discount).

● Adriatica Line: It's significant perhaps that this, the only Italian-owned company still surviving in these cut-throat waters, found it commercially necessary to bring its main Greek operation to Brindisi, rather than remain in Venice — its home port. An all-year-round service with three sailings weekly (rising to a peak of two a day) to **Patras** via Corfu and Igoumenitsa. Stopover at Corfu usually permitted. Duration 17-19 hours. Three of the larger (7,000 ton) ships on this route, with swimming pool, *Appia* (15kts), *Espresso Grecia* (19kts). and the recently introduced *Kypros Star*. UK agent: Sealink UK, address as above.

● Fragline: A daily service between April and October to **Patras** via Corfu and Igoumenitsa. Stopover permitted at Corfu. Duration 19 hours. Two medium sized ships, *Eolos* (3,000 tons) and *Ouranos* (4,000 tons). UK agent: Viamare Travel, address as above.

● Hellenic Mediterranean Lines: A three times weekly service (rising to twice daily) between March and December to **Patras** via Corfu and Igoumenitsa and during the summer peak one of its ships makes an additional call at Sami, **Kefallonia.** Stopover permitted at Corfu only. Duration 17-19 hours. Three average sized ships (4-5,000 tons), *Egnatia, Lydia* and *Corinthia* or *Poseidonia.* UK agent: Viamare Travel, address as above.

● Anco Ferries: A three times weekly service (rising to daily) between March and October to **Patras,** with a call at Igoumenitsa during a few summer weeks. Duration 17 hours. In addition to its own *Flavia* (4,000 tons) the company uses Hellenic Cypriot Mediterranean Line's slightly smaller *Valentino.* These ships might be attractive to owners of caravans and campers since, if these are stowed on an open part of the cardeck, their use for sleeping or refreshment is permitted during the passage. UK agent: Amathus Holidays, 51 Tottenham Court Road, London W1P 0HS.

● Agapitos Lines: This company has deployed up to three medium sized ferries in the Adriatic — *Corfu Sea, Corfu Sky* and *Corfu Diamond* (with swimming pool) — in addition to its more numerous Aegean operations; but currently only the latter seems to be running, on a limited basis, to **Patras** with calls at Corfu and

Ouranos *(Fragline), employed on the short haul route between Brindisi and Patras.*

Igoumenitsa, on alternate days during three of the summer months. Stopover permitted at Corfu. Duration 20 hours. In view of possible future uncertainty, enquiry would best be made to the UK agent: Viamare Travel, address as above.

● Nausimar Ferries: Despite this use of the plural the company owns but a single smallish ferry, *Hellenic Spirit,* which shuttles three times weekly (rising to daily) to **Igoumenitsa,** with a call at Corfu, between June and October. Duration 17½ hours.

● Seven Islands Shipping and Tourist: This summer service is highly advantageous to those wanting to visit a number of Ionian islands, since on its way to **Patras** it calls at Corfu, Igoumenitsa, Paxos, **Ithaka** and **Kefallonia,** whilst stopover is permitted at all of these islands (only the normal port fees being payable for this facility). Moreover passengers booked to go no further than Kefallonia are permitted a free connection to either **Zakynthos** or **Levkas** by local ferry boat. An alternate day service (rising to daily for much of the period) between June and September. The company does not itself own the ships on this route but charters them each year — currently *Ionis* (16kts, 100 cars) from Hellenic Coastal Lines and *Ionian Glory* (18kts, 220 cars) from Strinzis. The latter is not ideal for the route, being too large to berth at Ithaka. Duration between Brindisi and Patras would be 21 hours, if any passenger were to stay on board throughout. Day to day operations are controlled by Seven Islands Travel, Argostoli, Kefallonia; and since the service is both unique and popular, reservation is advisable. The Brindisi agent is Pattimare.

● Hellenic Cruising Holidays: In 1988 this company inaugurated a new three times weekly service to **Preveza,** calling at Corfu and Paxos, during July and August. Their ferry is the brand new *M/V Remvi* (700 tons, capacity 16 cars and 350 passengers, air-conditioned), thus distinguished as the smallest ferry now crossing the Adriatic. Nevertheless it proved popular that first year, so its operating period will probably be extended somewhat in 1989. Preveza is very convenient for **Levkas,** where the Agent is Scorpio Travel. Agent in Brindisi: Brinmare.

From Bari

Not only is Bari a more attractive city than Brindisi, but its small compact port is a pleasure to use. The increased distance to Greece may well be compensated by a shorter journey in Italy, whereas fares and discounts are comparable with Brindisi. Two shipping lines use the port, only one of whom operates to Greece. This is:

● Ventouris Ferries: A service to **Patras** runs practically all year round with three services a week (rising to daily). *Grecia Express* (3,000 tons) sails direct, whereas the faster *Athens Express* (6,000 tons) calls at Corfu and Igoumenitsa during Easter and summer peaks. Duration 19 to 21 hours. In summer a third ship, *Patra Express* (3,500 tons), shuttles between Bari and Igoumenitsa, calling at Corfu. UK agent: Viamare Travel, address as above.

From Otranto

This is one of the prettiest little ports in Italy, and the nearest to Greece; were it able to take larger ships no doubt it would be used by other operators. As it is, it has only:

● R Line: The company has been operating since 1964, and claims to offer the cheapest crossing. The service runs between June and September, initially three sailings weekly (rising during two peak weeks to a daily service) to **Igoumenitsa** with a call at Corfu. Their ship is the *Roanna* (1,400 tons, and thus second smallest across the Adriatic). Duration 10 to 14 hours. UK agent: Viamare Travel, address as above.

From Yugoslavia

For independent travellers already in Yugoslavia, there is a sea route to the Ionian islands additional to the peak season one already mentioned under Strinzis above:

● Jadrolinija: This company operates a service along the Yugoslav coast, which extends during the summer half of the year to Corfu and **Igoumenitsa**, with 1-3 sailings weekly. Suitable ports for embarkation include Rijeka, Split, Korcula, Dubrovnik and Bar. Duration (Dubrovnik to Igoumenitsa) 20 hours. The company has three ships, *Slavia I* and *Liburnija* (both 3,000 tons), and the smaller *Ilirija* (2,000 tons) which normally remains in home waters. Fares are denominated in US dollars, so overcoming the inflationary tendencies of the local currency. UK agent: Yugotours, Chesham House, 150 Regent Street, London W1R 5FA.

By private transport

Motoring within Greece, and the overland journey there, are covered in more detail in the next chapter. This section discusses the road journey through Italy, and entry and departure procedures at the ports.

The head of the Fiskardo inlet, with the arrival of the car ferry **Kostis Kafafis,** *since succeeded by the similar Aphrodite L.*

Driving through Italy

The Italian *autostrade* form one of the best motorway networks in Europe - which is just as well since many important trunk roads *(strade statale)* are quite inadequate for the amount of traffic they have to carry. The main areas of concern to motorists hurrying through Italy to catch their ferry will probably be fuel and motorway tolls.

Fuel Italian petrol, at 1360 lire/litre (about £2.65 per gallon) is the most expensive in Western Europe, and the authorities have a complicated scheme for mitigating its effects on tourism. This can be made use of once each calendar year by overseas residents visiting Italy in privately-owned foreign registered cars. Motorcaravans should also be eligible, but diesel and LPG vehicles, their fuel being substantially cheaper in Italy, are not entitled.

The scheme is designed around four packages of increasing value, structured to tempt motorists to spend more time in the less developed south. But most Ionian-bound motorists should find the first and smallest package ('Pacchetto Italia') sufficient for their (return) journey, even as far as Otranto, provided they enter Italy with a full fuel tank. The package costs about £70, payable in foreign currency (most common currencies are accepted), and consists of 12 petrol coupons each worth 15,000 lire, exchangable at major petrol stations throughout the country. Each coupon buys about 11 litres (2½ gallons), at a cost equivalent to a 15 per cent discount on pump prices. A further 7 per cent is gained in the form of a free issue of motorway toll vouchers worth 10,000 lire. Additional benefits of these packages include free breakdown service through ACI (the Automobile Club d'Italia), use of a free replacement car under certain circumstances following breakdown or accident, and a free map of Italy.

The package can be purchased through motoring organisations abroad, but also from ACI offices at the main frontier entry points — which also provide a refund on any unused coupons.

Motorways Tolls are payable on most Italian *autostrade,* except in the vicinity of the largest cities, and some sections in the south of the country. The normal procedure is to pick up a ticket from an automatic machine as you enter the system, and present it to an attendant at the exit barrier, where the amount to be paid is flashed onto a screen. You can use your free coupons for payment, and also banknotes of the principal foreign currencies (any change will be given in lire). But it must be said that the system has not yet adjusted to Greece's membership of the Common Market; so you might well have a struggle to convince the attendant that your surplus drachmae notes do, in fact, count as a principal foreign currency.

Speed limits These are normally 110 kmh on main roads outside of built-up areas, and 140 kmh on motorways. However a new law designed to reduce the very high rate of accidents at weekends was recently introduced, with the effect that during this period limits become 20 kph lower. Traffic police, who are empowered to impose on-the-spot fines, are making a great show of enforcement, from which foreigners are not immune.

Theft Thundering down the motorway, preoccupied with problems of petrol coupons, motorway tolls, and getting to the port in time to catch the ferry, it's very easy to overlook the vital matter of the security of your vehicle and its contents. Italy has the worst record of any European country for thefts from motor vehicles, and many a foreign vehicle has been broken into at motorway service stations, sometimes even when the occupants were asleep inside. More dangerous still is the moment when you have just arrived at the port, and need to go off for some purpose such as buying a ticket.

C/F Paxi *in her customary berth near the north mole of the harbour.* **Paxi** *may be a minnow among car ferries, but she's invaluable for making a day excursion to the ruins of ancient Olympia, via the mainland port of Katakolon.*

A foreigner's car left unattended for even a couple of minutes is at great risk; try and leave a capable looking adult inside, with the means of locking him/herself in. If that is not possible, drive into the port area, and leave the vehicle locked where the police can see it; come back as soon as you can. You have been warned!

Port formalities Apart from the little local difficulty already mentioned in connection with Brindisi, and the ever-present problem of being one among too many others at peak periods, motorists should have no difficulty in passing through the formalities prior to boarding their ferry. Naturally you will ensure that you have passport, ticket, and boarding card ready for inspection, and can lay your hands on vehicle registration documents, green card and driving licence. (For the older green UK licence, an Italian translation is technically required, which you can obtain through the motoring organisations. Alternatively you can arrange with the DVLC Swansea to exchange your green for the new pink licence which, conforming as it does to the European Community model, should be completely acceptable throughout the EEC.)

Entry and departure formalities at Greek ports

These are in fact little more onerous than in Italy, but they may well seem so owing to language difficulties and the more alien atmosphere. Documentation is covered in more detail in the next chapter, but the main difference is a procedure aimed at preventing foreigners from selling their cars (as well as some expensive items like colour television sets, which, together with large amounts of foreign currency, should also be declared) which would fetch much higher prices in Greece than in Western Europe. Motorists must therefore fill up a simple form on entry and exit, giving basic details about themselves and their vehicle. This form is handed in to the police, who will return the counterfoil, stamped, and at the same time stamp an entry on an empty page at the back of the passport. The counterfoil needs to be handed over at the port gate (or on boarding the ferry for the return journey). Information on the forms is subsequently entered on computer. Provided you leave within three months, your exit form will produce a suitable second stamp on your passport, as well as a matching computer entry. If that does not happen, the police will start looking for you and the vehicle!

Presumably this formality will be phased out after 1992.

By rail and by bus

This topic is covered in the next chapter. For present purposes it is only necessary to select a route passing through Italy (rather than Yugoslavia), such as the Parthenon Express from Paris. These will inevitably make use of one of the ferries mentioned above, probably from Brindisi to Patras. Thereafter proceed from your Greek arrival port to the islands, as discussed below.

Departure points for the islands

By now you should have a good idea of which route you want to take to the island of your choice. Here is more information about the points of departure. In sequence from north to south they are:

Preveza
This pleasant town of some 12,000 inhabitants is the departure point for **Levkas** (only a 20-minute ride from the airport on a special bus), which is itself a departure point for **Ithaka** and **Kefallonia** (see details in next section). Preveza is strung out along the sheltered shore of the Ambracian Gulf — joined to the sea indeed, but more resembling a vast inland lagoon. The south end of the town terminates in one of the pair of sandy peninsulas enclosing the bay; on the other, opposite, only 1km distant, stands the small village of Aktion with its Venetian fort. In Latin times when called Actium it gave its name to the great sea battle of antiquity in which the fleets of Anthony and Cleopatra were routed by that of Octavian in 31 BC.

There are several campsites to the north of the town, among which Monolithi Camping, situated beside a vast sandy beach some 8kms distant, is perhaps the most satisfactory.

Small open deck car ferries cross between Preveza and Aktion every 20 minutes (every half hour from 2200, and every hour between midnight and 0600). Fare 29drs passengers, 281drs car. Duration of trip 5 minutes. Plans exist to build a road bridge.

Two kilometres south of Aktion the road makes a detour to run round the perimeter of Preveza (Aktion) Airport, which receives international charter flights from the UK and other countries, and domestic flights from Athens and (sometimes) Corfu. An Olympic

Airways bus takes domestic passengers to Preveza town from here, using the ferry. A KTEL bus meets most scheduled flights for the benefit of passengers for Levkas. Charter flights are met by tour operator's buses; taxis are also available. The airport is shared with the military, so photos must not be taken.

Levkas

Although technically an island by virtue of the man-made canal that separates it from the mainland, this island status is ambiguous, especially since recent changes have made the canal only an insignificant obstacle to vehicles. For nowadays it is straddled by a pontoon bridge, which closes occasionally to open the channel for ships to pass through. Motorists are unlikely to be delayed for more than a few minutes, if at all. So because Levkas is a departure point for **Ithaka** and **Kefallonia** and its ports can be reached by road regardless of weather conditions or the availability of ferries, for the purposes of this chapter it has been treated as if part of the mainland.

Levkas town is encountered shortly after crossing the bridge. Although caiques from the town do make excursions down the canal in summer, even as far as Kefallonia and Ithaka, for present purposes one continues beyond it down the east coast to one of the two other ports of Levkas:

● **Nidri** 17 kms from Levkas town, is the departure port for **Ithaka, Kefallonia,** and the small island of **Meganisi.** Until recently there was an open deck car ferry service just to Meganisi island, 2-6 times daily all year round (20mins). But the arrival of a second and larger ferry boat created spare capacity, and so an additional service to small ports in the north of Kefallonia and Ithaka was initiated in 1988. At 0830 the *F/B Meganisi* leaves on a triangular circuit: Fiskardo (1hrs) — Frikes (40mins) — Nidri (1hr 20mins). Fares (Nidri to Fiskardo): passengers 371drs, cars 2041drs. At 1500 a second circuit begins, but in the reverse sequence, usually by the slightly smaller *F/B Levkas.* It was intended that this Fiskardo-Frikes service should run every day, all year round; but in the event during October frequency was reduced to twice weekly, and it was expected to stop completely for the period November to March.

● **Vassiliki,** 34kms from Levkas town, is the departure port for **Kefallonia** (Fiskardo and Sami). The service linking Levkas with Ithaka and Kefallonia was pioneered here, when an open deck car ferry named *Kostas Kafafis* started operations in May 1984. This has since been replaced by the similar but newer *F/B Aphrodite L,* now based in Sami. No doubt it was intended to continue the three island link, but owing presumably to competition from the Nidri ferry Ithaka is not now visited — though it may be again in future seasons. In 1988 the ferry left Vassiliki twice daily for Fiskardo (50mins) and Sami (½hr) between the beginning of June and the end of September. Fares (Vassiliki to Fiskardo): passengers 319drs, cars 1320 drs. *Aphrodite L* is owned and operated by Seven Islands Travel of Argostoli.

Part of the quayside at Nidri, used by the open-deck car ferries **Meganisi** *and* **Nidri** *for their services to Meganisi island, Frikes (Ithaka) and Fiskardo (Kefallonia).*

Chapter 12 contains further amplification of some of these topics, details of buses from Levkas town to Nidri and Vassiliki, as well as a full discussion of Meganisi and other minor islands close to Levkas.

Astakos

This small town of some 3,000 inhabitants, at the head of a long sheltered bay, is the departure port for **Ithaka** (Vathy) and **Kefallonia** (Ag. Efemia). During the Wars of Independence in the 1820s it was used as an operational base by the Greeks under Sir Richard Church, when it was known as Dragomestre. No doubt he relied on its isolation to help protect his forces against overland attack — the problem of its poor land communications has continued little changed until quite recently. Then at the end of the 1970s work began on driving a broad new road up the coast to Mitikas — a section that until then was virtually non-existent. And in 1984, shortly after this was completed, a new ferry service with Kefallonia was initiated. This is operated by a small conventional car ferry of Italian origin called *Thiaki* (500tons), based in Ag. Efemia in Kefallonia, which belongs to the Pnoe Shipping Company of Piraeus. It leaves Ag. Efemia every morning, calling at Ithaka (Vathi) 1½hrs later, and reaches Astakos after 3½ hours, where a bus for Patras is waiting for it; it returns by the same route in early afternoon. Fares to Kefallonia: passengers 590drs, cars 3041drs. The service continues all the year, but naturally has to be suspended occasionally, usually during winter, for repairs or maintenance.

Patras

Patras is a departure port for **Kefallonia** and **Ithaka.** The town faces westwards, and from it you can sometimes see the nearer Ionian islands, perhaps silhouetted against a sunset across the waters of the Gulf of Patras. It is the third largest town in Greece, and a busy centre for commerce and industry. Its focus is the port, which is large and in a seemingly continual state of extension — in spite of which facilities have not kept pace with the ever-increasing number of ships which use it, nor all the extra passenger and vehicle traffic generated by their ever-greater size.

The **port** has vehicle entrances towards its two extremities. When last reshaped it was intended that the north entrance (towards Athens) should be reserved exclusively for all the international traffic. Entrance is therefore through a large low concrete-pillared building, which contains customs, police and passport control, and a number of small sub-offices belonging to the main agents for each of the shipping lines, from which you obtain your boarding pass. Inside there are also money changing facilities, the smallest of the town's three OTE telephone offices, telephone kiosks for when the

OTE is closed, and (beyond the customs area) a duty-free shop. All of these adjust their hours to be open at those times when ships are embarking and disembarking passengers. Right at the entrance to the building is a small and very useful NTOG information office, open 0700-2130 Monday-Saturday and 1400-2030 Sunday. Until recently the main regional office of the NGOT was in the same building; it has now moved to cooler and more spacious premises in the northern outskirts, 2kms up the coast road, on the first floor of 110 Iroon Politechniou. Just outside the port entrance is a post office, keeping normal postal service hours, which can change Giro and Eurocheques.

The tiny caique harbour of Pessades, with the lower slopes of Mt Ainos behind. The ferry **Mana Barbara** *uses a concrete apron for embarkation, just out of picture, bottom right.*

Outside the port gates Iroon Politechniou becomes one-way in a southerly direction — as it goes round the first bend it changes its name to Othonas Amalias. The first inland road parallel with it, Ag. Andreou (merging into Ag. Dionissiou), takes traffic in the opposite direction; but wait for the street called Norman before turning off it towards the port, or you risk going round in circles. Between the port entrance and the town centre, practically all the buildings accommodate **tourist agencies** anxious to sell you ferry tickets for Italy. If you know which line you want to travel by, you can find the office of the main agent by walking along and looking out for a large board with the name of your shipping company or its ferries. But if you have not committed yourself it is better to visit one of those few agencies which represent all the lines and can sell you a ticket for any of them. One such is Giannatos Travel-Tourism at 15 Othonos Amalias, where good English is spoken and the staff are patient and friendly.

The **north terminal** was built to service the dozen international ferries then using Patras — since when their numbers have increased to more than 30! Consequently at peak periods the crush of passengers and vehicles converging on the building became impossible to handle there, and it was necessary to take emergency measures until such time as the current phase of extension is finished. Two international lines Kareogeorgis from Ancona and Ventouris from Bari were therefore transferred to the **south port** which had hitherto handled domestic ferries only, and the offices of their main agents are now situated outside the south gate of the port on Othonos Amalias. This is not the penance it might seem. For although facilities there are less modern they do include a spacious police and customs hall (100m beyond the police on the gate), adjoined by another duty-free shop. (Prices and range of goods sold in both duty free shops compare favourably with what is available on the ships.) But above all the formalities here take place in less stressful surroundings, since normally only one international ship is embarking at a time.

Loosely defining the boundary between the north and south parts of the port is a long broad pier which projects deeply into the harbour. Along this the citizens of Patras are accustomed to take their evening *volta,* which they do regardless of the swirling stream of cars and lorries in the process of embarking and disembarking. The police are understandably touchy about the possibility of goods bought from the duty-free shops being passed back into the country, so they do their best to enforce some segregation.

Domestic ferry services also use the south port, normally in the vicinity of the central pier. These run throughout the year to Sami (Kefallonia) and Vathi (Ithaka), and in summer also to Paxos and Corfu, but it is impossible to predict details until the end of the previous year, because of competition between rival shipping companies for permission to operate on the route. Traditionally

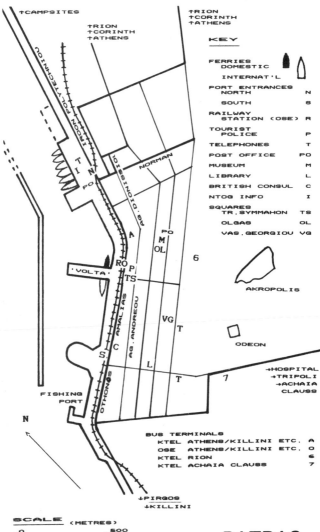

PATRAS

services leave daily at 1330, so giving comfortable time for passengers to arrive from Athens, even if travelling by rail. A fixture to Sami and Vathi for much of the year is likely to be Strinzis Line's *Kefallinia*. Except between June and September when it's engaged on Seven Islands Travel's international service to Brindisi, the *Ionis* too will probably operate (in competition) on the same route, extending it once a week or more to Paxos and Corfu. Other contenders may well come forward in future years. Duration to Sami 3½hrs; to Vathi 5½hrs. Fares to Sami (those to Ithaka are only a little more): passengers 1025drs, cars 4266drs +.

There are, by the way, legal obstacles preventing ferry companies from transporting passengers on a domestic sector of an international route. In other words if you want to travel in summer on the *Ionis* or *Ionian Glory* between Patras and any of the Greek islands, you need a valid ticket to Brindisi to do so legitimately. The requirement is actually illegal under EEC rules, so might be revoked before long.

A hydrofoil service which once operated between Patras, Kefallonia and Zakynthos was abandoned when the operator transferred his craft to the Aegean.

Opposite the pier, on the other side of Orthonas Amalias is **Platia Trion Symmahon,** one of the main squares of Patras, and liberally furnished with groups of tables and chairs belonging to the several cafs surrounding it. One corner of this square is dominated by the Patras head office of the **National Bank of Greece:** in addition to normal banking hours it opens from 1100-1300 on Saturdays and Sundays, as well as every evening from 1730-2000, which can be very convenient for changing foreign currency. The tourist police are alongside, facing the port.

Opposite the National Bank on the port side of Orthonas Amalias is the **railway station.** The presence of this railway line and its trains which clatter and grind their way through the very centre of Patras is unhelpful in solving the complexities of traffic management in this congested area! The Peloponnese railway is mentioned in the next chapter: sufficient here to say that only those with time on their hands are likely to want to travel on it, since the buses are so much quicker. But immediately outside the station is an extensive bus stop where, amongst others, Athens buses for Kefallonia and Zakynthos pause on their way to the Killini ferries. OSE (railway, see next chapter) buses for Athens also load their passengers here. The KTEL bus station which also serves Athens is 200m further north, a conspicuous building on the bend of Orthonos Amalias.

Northwards from the port the coast road (Iroon Politechniou) comes to a dead end after 5kms, at the entrance to the NTOG's Ag. Patron **campsite**. The site is well laid out, like all NTOG campings, with tents and caravans segregated, each with spacious and well-defined pitches and use of the private beach. It remains more or less open throughout the year. An adjoining beach is also administered by NTOG. About 2kms nearer to the port is Cavouri Camping, a smaller, simpler and slightly cheaper campsite, though more than adequate for a short-term stay. This is situated behind the Cavouri Restaurant, both of them prominently signposted from the adjoining coast road. Open April to October.

Killini

The small port of Killini is a departure port for **Kefallonia** and **Zakynthos,** and for interchange between them. It lies about 80kms south west of Patras, whence it is reached from the New National Road. This begins 3kms south of Patras — at present there is no fast link with the Athens-Patras National Road, but neither are any tolls levied on the New Road. The first turning off to Killini is at Lehena (poorly signposted), but the next is a better road. At Neohorion take the right fork whatever the signposting, otherwise you end up at Killini Loutra (a sulphur waters spa and hotel complex), with a 15km journey back to the port.

The bus from Athens can be boarded outside the Patras railway station, and the journey to Killini takes about an hour. Select a bus whose destination is your chosen island and which goes all the way across on the ferry with you (see next chapter), and the ferry will wait. There are also buses direct to Killini from the Patras KTEL bus terminal which cross to Zakynthos.

It is possible also to take the Patras-Pirgos train and change to a branch line for Killini at Kavasila — an insignificant junction easily missed. Allow 4hrs for this regardless of what the timetable says — experienced local people jokingly advise 8!

Ferries for Kefallonia and Zakynthos berth at the same jetty, and it's sometimes arranged that the two ships are in port at the same time, to facilitate interchange between them. Each line has a small ticket office at the side of the embarkation area, which opens to sell tickets shortly before its ferry is due. There should be a board outside giving current timings.

Apart for an excursion service from Katakolon (described below) Killini is the only mainland departure port for Zakynthos. The island shipowner's cooperative (Kinopraxis Pleion) currently owns four good-sized conventional car ferries (1,000-2,000 tons) which maintain an effective all year service. Duration 1¼hrs, normal frequency 3-7 services daily, with extra unscheduled trips when traffic justifies. Fares: passengers 416drs, cars 2303drs.

To Kefallonia there are two lines. The longer-established route to Poros is operated by Strinzis Line's medium-sized conventional car ferry *Ainos* (1,200 ton). Duration 1½hrs, frequency 1-3 times daily all year subject to repair or maintenance requirements. Fares: passengers 536drs, cars 2922drs. Recently a new service to the capital Argostoli has been initiated with the medium-sized conventional car ferry *Argostoli*. Like the *Ionis* this is owned by Hellenic Coastal Lines and operated by Seven Islands Travel. Duration 2¾hrs, frequency 1-2 times daily all year subject to repair or maintenance requirements. Fares: passengers 872drs, cars 3428drs +.

Killini has basic hotel and restaurant facilities, a few shops, petrol station and a post office. The nearest campsites are situated some distance the other side of Killini Loutra, but short-term free camping on the beach is quite possible, apart from some difficulty in finding shade. There is a water tap in the port.

Katakolon

Only a couple of decades ago when many roads in the Peloponnese were still in a deplorable condition, Katakolon was an important port of call on the ferry service between Patras and Kalamata, which had hitherto been the best means of travel up and down the coast. Today it is useful as the nearest port to the major archeological tourist attraction at Olympia, and cruise liners call to send their passengers on excursion there. These include the luxury cruise ferry *Orient Express* (see above), in which it is possible to return to Venice once weekly throughout its operating season.

It is also visited three times weekly between April and October by the small conventional car ferry *Paxi* (12 vehicles) from **Zakynthos** town — a good example of a ferry service developed to meet the needs of tourists rather than island residents. It is owned by Zante Tours, which operates it on a regular weekly schedule to Katakolon and Kefallonia (Poros), where a coach meets it to continue the excursion. The present ship is rather elderly, but there are plans to replace it with another in 1989.

Travel between the islands

All but one of the car ferries operating between the South Ionian islands have now been introduced. The exception is a medium-sized open deck ferry called *Mana Barbara,* which for much of the year scratches a modest living as one of several operating the frequent daily service across the broad bay of Argostoli, from Lixourion to the capital of Kefallonia. During the summer it goes solo to provide the shortest crossing between *Kefallonia* and *Zakynthos,* using the tiny ports of Pessades and Skinari. Duration about 1½hrs, frequency twice daily in July and August, twice on three days of the week in June and September.

The threads can now be drawn together, and all the possibilities for hopping direct from island to island in the South Ionian can be summarised (from now on Levkas is again treated as an island). Since Kefallonia is involved in all of them, they are listed port by port as departures from Kefallonia. For more extensive details see above and the individual island chapters in Part 2.

The open-deck car ferry **Agios Gerasimos** *approaching the Lixouri ferry berth at Argostoli. The very similar* **Mana Barbara** *forsakes this internal route in summer to provide a link between Pessades (Kefallonia) and Skinari (Zakynthos).*

Summary of inter-island travel
From Kefallonia to Levkas
- Sami and Fiskardo to Vassiliki. *C/F Aphrodite L.*
  2 x daily June to September.
- Fiskardo via Frikes (Ithaka) to Nidri. *C/F Meganisi.*
  2 x daily April to September. 2 x 3 days a week in October.

From Kefallonia to Ithaka
- Fiskardo to Frikes. *C/F Meganisi.*
  Daily April to September.   3 x weekly in October.
- Ag. Efemia to Vathi. *C/F Thiaki.*
  Daily for much of the year.
- Sami to Vathi. *C/F Ionis, C/F Kefallinia* etc.
  About 2 x daily all year.

From Kefallonia to Zakynthos
- Poros to Zakynthos town. *C/F Paxi.*
  2-3 weekly between April and October.
- Pessades to Skinari. *C/F Mana Barbara.*
  2 x daily July and August.   2 x 3 days a week June
  and September.
- Argostoli to Zakynthos town.

In past years there have been a few summer sailings by *C/F Martha* (part of the Kinopraxis Pleion), whose future is presently uncertain.

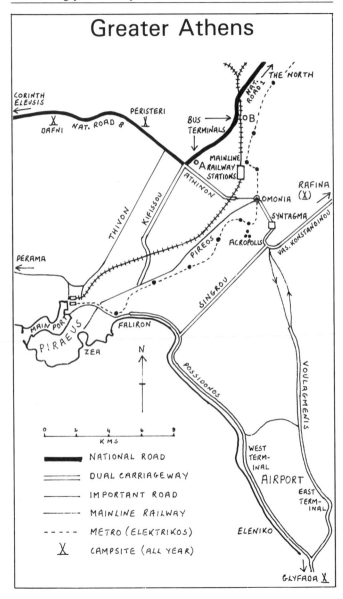

Greater Athens

FOUR

Via Athens

Modern Greece is a surprisingly centralised society, where practically all political and economic decisions of consequence are made in the capital. For this reason important dignitaries from the provinces and islands must continually visit it. What's more, many people in Athens live there only because of their need for work: they do not consider themselves properly Athenian, but rather natives of wherever they originally came from — and until circumstances permit their permanent return, they and their families lose no opportunity to go back for feast days, holidays and family occasions. To meet these needs efficient transport links have developed over the years between Athens and the islands.

For similar reasons Athens finds itself with more, better and sometimes cheaper facilities for international travel than anywhere else in Greece. Thus it can make good sense to travel to the Greek islands by way of Athens, especially for those who want to see more of Greece. This chapter therefore discusses Greater Athens, its various arrival and departure points and how best to move around the city between them; how to get there from outside Greece (but excluding those routes already described in the previous chapter); and gives details of the various routes for getting away to your chosen destination.

Greater Athens

Like most capitals, Athens can seem vast and confusing to the first time visitor. It is certainly true that the modern city sprawls over a huge area, and that some 3.3 million people — one third of the total population of the country — live there. But tourists passing through need only to think in terms of the city centre and their arrival and departure points be they by ship, rail, bus or aeroplane. Thus there are five areas of interest:

- Athens, city centre.
- Athens airport, at Elinco.
- Piraeus, port of Athens.
- Athens, main line railway stations.
- Athens, long distance bus terminals.

Moving around Athens

Taxis These are plentiful and relatively cheap. However, because of regulations introduced to lessen smog in the city, private motor cars can only be used on alternate days — according to whether their registration ends with an odd or an even number. Consequently car owners must find an alternative method of getting to work — and so many appropriate the taxis.

On the other hand it's quite in order to stop any passing taxi with an empty seat that seems to be going in the right direction, and ask to be taken along. You still have to pay as if you had it all to yourself — thus taxi drivers tend to be more enthusiastic about sharing than your fellow passengers. Few drivers are proficient in foreign languages, and the official tariff is complicated; so it can happen that both the place the driver expects you to get out and the fare he demands can come as disagreeable surprises. Even so, taxis — if you can obtain one — may well be faster and more convenient than other public transport, even if more expensive.

Buses The metropolitan network is run by three independent operators, whose activities are coordinated by the supervising authority OAS. Buses come in all colours of the rainbow, each having its own significance. Ordinary city buses belong to EAS, are coloured **blue,** and normally function between 0500 and midnight. Fares are a flat 30drs per journey irrespective of distance. Frequent checks are made by uniformed inspectors, so tickets need to be kept, but early morning travel before 0800 is free. The **green** bus service differs from the blue only in that it is run by ISAP, whose main function is organising the underground railway. **Orange** buses go outside Athens to other towns within Attica. There are also **yellow trolley** buses, which mostly circulate within the centre, operated by ILPAP. These are not to be confused with the **yellow (express)** buses, now reduced to a single route between the airport(s) and Piraeus. The other yellow express bus routes were replaced in the summer of 1988 by a new Express Bus system linking the two long distance bus terminals with the airport, via the city centre and

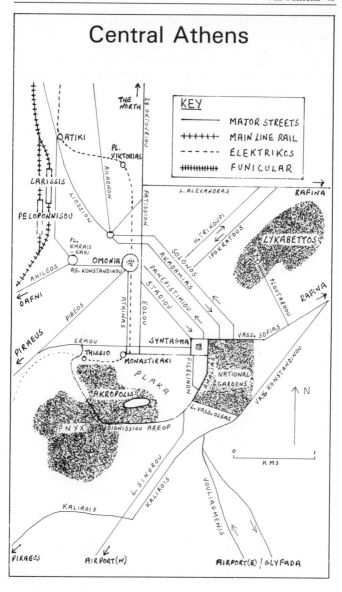

railway stations. These buses are double deckers, of a type well known to Londoners, but painted **blue and white** with a yellow stripe. Line A starts from bus terminal A, line B from bus terminal B. Those going to the Airport West (Olympic Airways) carry a diagonal red stripe across the A or B on their destination indicator: those for the Airport East (International) have a plain A or B. The fare for all the express buses is 100drs (150drs between midnight and 0600). Though less than you would pay for a similar service in western Europe, it is much more than on other buses; but special provision is made for tourist luggage and, because of fewer intermediate stops, they do get there quicker.

Athenians are enthusiastic bus users, so their buses are often crowded. Another difficulty for foreigners is to work out which route number to take. These are listed at the bus stops *(stasis)*, together with their destinations — but naturally in Greek.

Underground railway A single route electric railway connects the north east suburb of Kifissia with Piraeus, via the city centre. Mostly it runs on the surface, though like the District lines in London, it does dive underground below the city centre. Athenians call it the *elektrikos,* and Metro is also understood. Fares are 30drs, as on the blue buses, and because ticket offices do not open until 0800, travel has likewise come to be regarded as free until that time. But increasingly stations are being automated; first you buy your ticket from a coin machine, then you must insert it into an automatic turnstyle — a tricky operation, so it may be best to stand aside and watch a local do it. Trains run between 0500 and midnight, about every 5 minutes on the section between Omonia and Piraeus (every 15 mins north of Omonia). Two new intersecting lines are at present under construction.

If there's a station near where you want to go, the Metro usually offers the quickest and most comfortable journey. Omonia in the centre, Monastiraki further south adjoining Plaka, and Thission, for the Acropolis, are stations useful to tourists.

Air travel

Athens airport
Athens has one airport, situated at Elenico, about 10kms south of the city centre, which is split between two completely separate and self-contained sets of terminal buildings. The East (International) terminal, used by all foreign airlines, leads off the main Athens-

Glyfada highway. The West terminal, used exclusively by Olympic Airways for both their domestic and international flights, is alongside the Piraeus-Glyfada coast road. Both terminals have a duty-free shop inside the departure building.

A tunnel under the runway to connect the two terminals does exist, but it has not been used for passengers since airports became vulnerable to international terrorism. Transfer between the two terminals is therefore by bus, running outside the perimeter fence, i.e.:

● Piraeus yellow express bus 19 every 30 mins (and every 1½hrs from midnight to 0600), which starts from the Airport (East).

● Olympic Airways shuttle bus (free to O.A. passengers), leaving the West Airport every hour on the hour, and the East Airport every hour on the half-hour.

Arrival from overseas

Flights arrive in Athens from all over the world: from London alone there are at least five scheduled services daily, as well as many charter flights from Gatwick and regional UK airports. Passengers will find themselves at the Airport (West) terminal only if they fly with Olympic Airways or its associated charter company; at the Airport (East) terminal if they fly with any other airline.

Athens Airport (East) The impressive-looking terminal was designed by the Finnish-American Eero Saarinen — besides some airport buildings in the USA he was also responsible for the American Embassy in Grosvenor Square, London. Unfortunately it has difficulty coping in high summer, among other reasons because of the many tourists who doss down in public spaces whilst waiting for late night flights. Arrivals are usually easier: but whilst waiting to pick up your luggage do not miss the chance to ask for advice or leaflets from the NTOG information desk — once past customs you'll not be able to go back there, nor to the equally helpful Olympic Airways information desk.

The terminal building is in three sections — arrivals, departures and, between them, charters. Outside the arrivals building a taxi rank stands directly opposite. On the left is the airport bus terminal, with a choice of connections within the city.

● To the city centre. Double decker express bus A and B (plain) every 20 mins (every half hour from midnight to 0600) to Syntagma and Omonia. Also blue bus 121 every 20 mins to Vassilis Olgas.

● To the mainline railway stations. Double decker express bus B (plain).

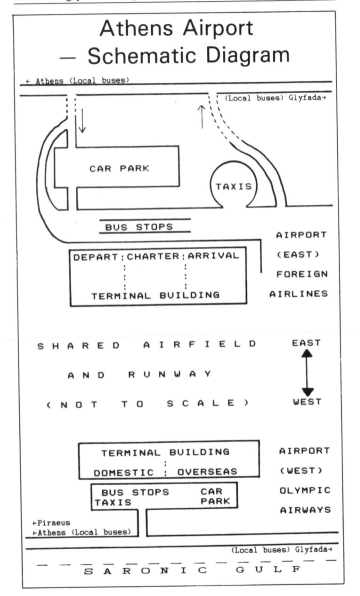

● To the long distance bus terminals. To terminal A, double decker express bus A (plain). To terminal B, double decker express bus B (plain).

● To Piraeus. Yellow express bus 19 every 20 mins (every 1½hrs from midnight to 0600), calling at the West Airport on the way. Also blue bus 101 to Klissovis/Theotaki.

Athens Airport (West) This is smaller than the East terminal, although extension work continues. Departures are on the right, and arrivals on the left, each with its domestic and international section. Many buses stop in the rather cramped forecourt, offering a choice of connections within the city.

● To the city centre. Double decker express bus A and B (red diagonal stripe) to Syntagma and Omonia. Olympic Airways bus every 30 mins to Syntagma (100drs). Blue bus 133 every half hour to Syntagma, also blue bus 122 every 20 mins to Vassilisis Olgas.

● To the mainline railway stations. Double decker express bus B (red diagonal stripe).

● To the long distance bus terminals. For terminal A, double decker express bus A (red diagonal stripe). For terminal B, double decker express bus B (red diagonal stripe).

● To Piraeus. Yellow express bus 19 on its way from the East Airport (see above for timing). Also blue bus 109 every 20 mins to Klissovis/Theotaki.

Departure to the islands

The following domestic flights are run by Olympic Airways from its Airport (West) terminal:

● To Kefallonia. 1-2 flights each day by Boeing 737. Duration 50mins.

● To Zakynthos. 1 flight each day by Boeing 737. Duration 40mins.

● To Preveza (Aktion) for Levkas. About 1 flight each day by Short 330 or the tiny Dornier 228. Duration 1hr 20mins.

Sea travel

Piraeus, port of Athens

The map of Piraeus shows the locations of the Customs House, Peloponissou and *elektrikos* railway stations, and the bus terminals that connect with other departure points. Tourist police patrol the area in summer — here in Piraeus their offices are integrated with

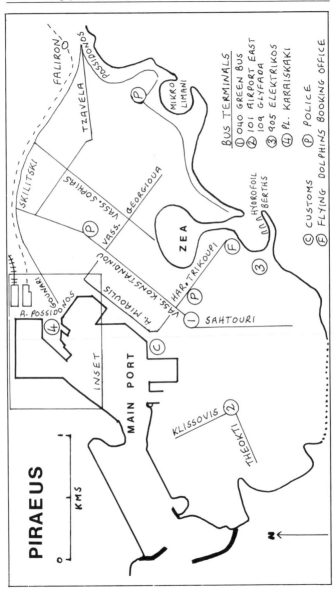

the municipal police. Another possible source of advice in summer is the port information kiosk. At other times you might try the Port Authority control desk, but the official probably does not speak English, even if he has the time.

Arrival from overseas

The table below summarises the various international scheduled services to Greece from within the Mediterranean and Black Seas (excluding those from Italy and Yugoslavia, see previous chapter). Virtually all are car ferries, apart from a few liners operated by the Russian Black Sea Company. Some services from the Near East are sensitive to the prevailing political situation.

from	between	duration	max. frequency
Cyprus	Limassol/Piraeus	31-65 hrs	at least weekly
Egypt	Alexandria/Piraeus	35-57 hrs	weekly
Israel	Haifa/Piraeus	45-59 hrs	several weekly
Syria	Latakia/Piraeus	78 hrs	occasional
	Tartous/Volos	(?)	weekly
Turkey	frequent connections via Greek Aegean islands of Chios, Kos, Lesbos, Rhodes and Samos.		

Connections within the city

● City centre. First choice is the *elektrikos*. Outside the rush hour green bus 040 to Filellion Street (Syntagma) leaving every 10 minutes day and night from Sakhtouri Street (1). Many buses to other parts.

● To the airport (East, International). Yellow express bus 19 from Akti Tselepi (Inset 1, the south side of shipping offices block on Karaiskaki Square) or Megara OLP (near the Customs House) every 20 mins (every 1½hrs from midnight to 0600). Also blue bus 101 from Klissovis/Theotaki (2).

● To the airport (West, Olympic Airways). Yellow express bus 19 on its way to the airport (East) — see above. Also blue bus 109 every 20 mins from Klissovis/Theotaki (2).

● To the mainline railway stations. By train from Peloponissou station (A), if there's one running. Otherwise via the city centre - Omonia *(elektrikos)* or Syntagma (green bus 040), then change.

● To the long distance bus terminals. Via the city centre, then change.

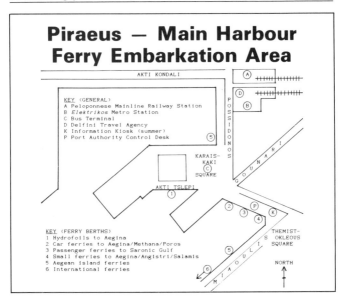

Piraeus — Main Harbour Ferry Embarkation Area

AKTI KONDALI

KEY (GENERAL)
A Peloponnese Mainline Railway Station
B *Elektrikos* Metro Station
C Bus Terminal
D Delfini Travel Agency
K Information Kiosk (summer)
P Port Authority Control Desk

KARAIS-
KAKI
SQUARE

AKTI TSLEPI

KEY (FERRY BERTHS)
1 Hydrofoils to Aegina
2 Car ferries to Aegina/Methana/Poros
3 Passenger ferries to Saronic Gulf
4 Small ferries to Aegina/Angistri/Salamis
5 Aegean island ferries
6 International ferries

THEMIST-
OKLEOUS
SQUARE

NORTH

Departure to the islands

Although it cannot quite be said that there are no connections by sea between Piraeus and the Ionian islands, they are to say the least tenuous! The luxury cruise ferry *Orient Express* passes through the Corinth Canal on its outward voyage from Venice before berthing at Piraeus; and on its return journey after rounding the Peloponnese it calls at Katakolon (see Chapter 3) for an excursion to Olympia. And if you define Kythira as an Ionian island, which is strictly correct, there are twice weekly car ferry connections there, as well as by hydrofoil (except in winter). But there are no onward sea connections from Kythira to the other Ionian islands, which is why it is not included in this volume.

Rail travel

Mainline railway stations

The two Athens railway stations are situated close together, about 1km north west of Omonia. Larissis, nearer to the centre, is the terminus for services from northern Greece, and indeed from the rest of Europe. About 200m beyond is Peloponissou, serving the Peloponnese: trains actually start at Piraeus, and run on a narrower 1 metre gauge. Note that all the long distance buses operated by OSE (the State railway) to destinations such as Patras, Thessaloniki and Corinth, leave from outside their appropriate station.

Arrival from overseas

Greece can be reached by rail from most European countries. From northern Europe this usually involves joining one of three named expresses:

● Venezia Express (Train 263). Dep Venice 1656, via Belgrade, arr Athens 0800 1½ days later.

● Hellas Express (Train D411). Dep Munich 2138, Zagreb, Belgrade, arr Athens 1330 1½ days later.

● Akropolis Express (Train D291). Dep Munich 0814, route as for Hellas Express, arr Athens 2300 1½ days later.

Travellers from Britain, perhaps the principal users of this book, can connect with any of these trains. Thus the total journey time from London to Athens is at least 2½ days. The cost of the ticket depends on whether the journey is via France, Belgium, or Holland (in order of increasing cost). Details, which very slightly with season, are as follows:

— Dep London (Victoria) 1430 via Dover, Calais, Paris, to Venice; thence by Venetia Express.

— Dep London (Liverpool Street) 1935 via Harwich and the Hook of Holland to Cologne (Köln); thence by Hellas Express .

— Dep London (Victoria) 1300 via Ostend and Köln to Munich; thence by Akropolis Express.

In practice, since prices for a normal return journey seem rather high (i.e. around £240 second class return) compared with the air fares, rail travel will probably be economic only for people under 26 years of age entitled to a monthly Inter-rail ticket or the two-monthly Transalpino ticket, and for senior citizens with British and European railcards.

All the above trains terminate at Larissis station.

Connections within the city

● To the city centre. Double decker express bus B (plain or diagonal red stripe) every 20mins (every 1½hrs from midnight-0600) to Omonia and Syntagma. Yellow trolley bus 1 every 10mins from 0500 to midnight to Omonia and Syntagma/Amalias.

● To the airport (East, International). Double decker express bus B (plain).

● To the airport (West, Olympic Airways). Double decker express bus B (red diagonal stripe).

● To the long distance bus terminals. To terminal B, double decker express bus B (plain or red diagonal stripe). To terminal A, probably safer via the city centre.

● To Piraeus. A train from Peloponissou would be convenient, but they are not frequent. Otherwise via Omonia and the *elektrikos,* or Syntagma (Filellion Street and green bus 040).

Departure for the islands
It is possible to achieve the first leg of this journey by rail, from the Peloponissou station to Patras or Killini. But for comments on this, and onward travel from the railhead see Chapter 3.

Bus travel

Long distance bus terminals.
Apart from the OSE buses (see railway stations above), most long distance buses in Greece are run by a pool of operators known as KTEL. In Athens they use two termini some 3kms from the centre, convenient to the motorways. **Terminal A** at 100 Kifissou Street, close to the motorway to Patras, serves the Peloponnese together with a majority of more distant destinations. **Terminal B** at 260 Liossion Street, near the motorway to Thessaloniki and 2kms north of terminal A, serves nearer destinations in the eastern half of central Greece.

Arrival from overseas
Well established and reputable companies such as Europabus, owned by rail companies, and Eurolines, of which National Express is a member, connect Athens with most countries of Western Europe. From London there are services most days which can take as little as 2½ days. Prices are around £135 return (1988). Cheaper fares can be found among private operators, some of which have been criticised in the past for inadequate safety standards; moreover the former leader among price cutters, Magic Bus, no longer operates from London. See advertisements in magazines such as *Time Out* for the current situation.

The bus journey is certainly arduous, even when its timings are adhered to. The duration of toilet stops can be quite inadequate for the number of passengers needing to use the often limited facilities

— although nowadays buses used as far as Yugoslavia (and possibly beyond) should have on board toilets. Food can be a problem: meals at the scheduled stopping places may be exhorbitantly expensive; and it sometimes happens that drivers try to prevent you from bringing your own food aboard their buses.

Most international bus services use Peloponissou railway station as their Athens terminal, but check with your chosen operator.

Connections within the city

● From terminal A. Double decker express bus A (plain or diagonal red stripe).

● From terminal B. Double decker express bus B (plain or diagonal red stripe).

Departure for the islands

A number of the ferries departing for Kefallonia and Zakynthos from Patras and Killini carry the Athens or Patras bus across to the island with them. The Kefallonia ferry from Patras should continue to Ithaka, but if you are going with it you need to tell the bus driver so that your luggage can be unloaded before he drives off in Kefallonia. The following buses from terminal A at 100 Kifissou Street go direct to the islands:

● For Zakynthos (via Killini). 2-3 daily, duration 7hrs. Fare 1485drs + ferry fare.

● For Kefallonia. 2-3 daily, duration 8hrs to Argostoli. Fare 2400drs + ferry fare.

● For Levkas. 3 daily, no ferry involved. Duration 7hrs. Fare 2000drs.

Alternatively you can take a bus to the port and choose your own ferry.

From terminal A at 100 Kifissou Street:

● For Patras. About hourly from 0630 to 2115. Fare 1130drs.

● For Astakos. Two daily, duration 5hrs. Fare 1610drs. The first bus at 0815 would be the best route to Ithaka.

Railway buses from Peloponissou railway station:

● For Patras. Some 20 buses between 0540 to 2120. Same price and duration as KTEL (terminal A).

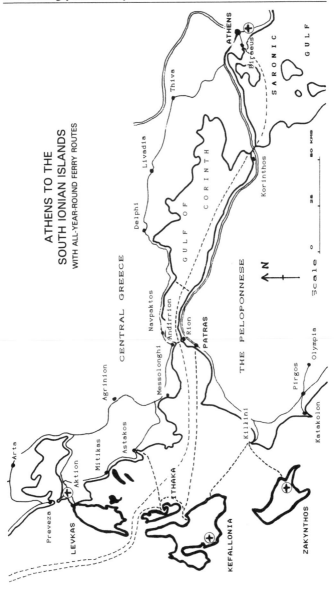

ATHENS TO THE
SOUTH IONIAN ISLANDS
WITH ALL-YEAR-ROUND FERRY ROUTES

By private transport

There is no real difficulty in driving across Europe overland to Greece, apart from the length of the journey — the distance between London and Athens, for example, being some 3,250kms (about 2,000 miles). The easiest route uses the new toll motorway through Austria from Salzburg to Klagenfurt. The main *autoput* (M1/E94-E5) through Yugoslavia is joined near Ljubljana. It is a flat and uninteresting road crowded with international juggernauts; much has now been reconstructed to full motorway standards, and new sections are regularly added; but parts of the remainder are in dangerously poor condition, especially north of Belgrade. That stretch can be bypassed by taking the M3 south west from Maribor through Osijek to join a good section of the autoput near Srem. Mitrovica — a slower but safer and more interesting route.

The coast road down the Adriatic is even more interesting, but 300kms longer. Being slow and winding, it is also somewhat dangerous. It is not at present possible to transit through Albania, and for political reasons there are sometimes restrictions on foreign motorists in the province of Kosovo.

Fuel coupons can be bought at the Yugoslav border, for payment in foreign currency. Regulations change in detail from year to year; only recently for example did it cease to be compulsory for foreigners to use coupons to buy fuel. These are available through foreign motoring organisations, or can be bought with foreign currency at the border. At the beginning of 1988 they had a nominal value of 1300 dinars, and entitled the motorist to an additional 5 per cent of fuel at standard prices (a complex procedure about which some pump attendants feign ignorance) but the current rate of inflation (250 per cent per year) is bound to give rise to further changes. Unused coupons can be refunded at a border, or through the Automobile Association of Yugoslavia (AMSJ) in Belgrade.

Documentation EEC nationals no longer require visas for up to six months' stay. Most other English-speaking tourists with valid national passports are entitled to a stay of three months. Vehicles are even more generously treated, since a 'Carnet de Passage en Douanes' is not necessary for periods of up to four months in Greece: instead, an entry is made in the driver's passport at the frontier. Even after four months, a banker's guarantee is an acceptable alternative to the 'Carnet'. An International Driving Permit is not needed by holders of British and several other European national driving licences; but an insurance 'Green Card', valid for Greece, is mandatory for all. Entry into Greece may well be refused if a passport contains the stamp of the Turkish Republic of Cyprus (Kibris).

Fuel (early 1989) The price of Super (96 octane), at 80drs/litre, is comparable with other countries in the area. Regular at 75drs/litre has the rather low octane value of 90. Diesel at 38drs/litre seems cheap. These prices are for Athens; elsewhere fuel costs 2-4drs/litre more, depending on distance from the refinery. There is as yet no price discounting, nor currently any petrol coupons scheme for tourists.

A few petrol stations are beginning to accept credit cards, and lead-free petrol *(amolibdi bensina)* is becoming available in some places.

Motorways The 'motorway' network, classified as National Road, extends from Evzoni on the Yugoslav border to Thessaloniki and Athens, and from Athens to Patras. The greater part is still single carriageway, although some upgrading work is in progress on busier sections. Some stretches of unimproved main road remain. Driving standards are relaxed, although by convention slower-moving traffic drives on the hard shoulder of single carriageways. Between Evzoni and Athens there are at present three toll sections — the first near Katerini (although another near Thessaloniki can be expected before long) — and two between Athens and Patras. Charges seem modest to foreigners — for example, about £1 for a private car between Evzoni and Athens. Tickets need to be retained for authentication within each toll section.

Road signs On main roads the road signs invariably appear in pairs. The first shows place names using the Greek alphabet, but is followed at about 100m by a second in the Roman alphabet. Numerals of course present no difficulty. All other road signs conform generally to normal European conventions. Turnings off towards campsites are almost always signposted from the main road.

Breakdowns and other requirements The Automobile and Touring Club of Greece (ELPA) operates a breakdown service in less remote parts of the country, free to foreigners who are members of their own national Automobile or Touring club. Assistance is obtained by dialling 104. In Athens and Thessaloniki this is a 24-hour service, elsewhere it is available between 0700 and 2200. It is obligatory to carry a warning triangle, first aid kit and a fire extinguisher. Seat belts must be worn where fitted. The maximum permitted level of alcohol in the bloodstream is low, at 0.05 per cent.

Campsites The following campsites in or near Athens remain open throughout the year:

● Athens Camping. At 189 Athinon Avenue, Peristeri, at the beginning of the Patras National Road. Nearest campsite to the city centre, with frequent buses there.

● Dafni Camping. At Dafni, on the Patras National Road about 3kms further from the city centre. Frequent buses.

● Dionissiotis Camping. On the Athens-Thessaloniki National Road, about 18kms from the city centre.

● Voula Camping. A NTOG-run site at Glyfada, a few kilometres south of the airport.

FIVE

Accommodation

Hotels

Greek hotels are strictly classified and supervised by the NTOG, in conjunction with the tourist police. The top grade, Luxury, is the only one unrestricted by any price control. Next come hotels graded A to E — although these gradings must be rather flexibly interpreted. The best rooms of the more popular hotels are often contracted to package operators. Some hotels offer 'bungalow' accommodation, sometimes self-catering, grouped around central facilities.

Conventional baths are rare in Greece, except in top grade hotels, and showers are the norm. Water heating is usually by solar panel, so showers are hotter in the evening. Towels and soap are normally provided.

Pensions

These are small purpose-built blocks of accommodation, usually with ensuite toilet and shower, and offered on a bed and breakfast basis (the breakfast is usually served at a nearby taverna). They offer cheaper and more flexible accommodation than hotels.

(Opposite) *Picturesque houses (most of them restored since the earthquake in 1953) in the village at Assos (Kefallonia) — a sheltered port of call for visiting yachts (see page 128).*

Service flats

These are blocks of accommodation suitable for self-catering. Standards of construction and finish are rather variable. The tourist agencies, usually positioned to intercept tourists as they stumble off the boat, will have the details.

Private accommodation

Privately owned houses — frequently described as **villas** — are often available for rent, and can give very good value for groups or families travelling together. Facilities will naturally include a kitchen. **Village rooms,** on the other hand, are simply for sleeping in. Typically these are within the house of a Greek family, although more and more are being purpose-built, sometimes with en suite shower and toilet or even some cooking facilities. Prices are controlled, and each room should contain a notice giving details. A room grade A is equivalent to a hotel room grade C, private grade B to hotel grade D, and private grade C to hotel grade E. The owner may be prepared to take less, out of season. Meals, if any, would be by private arrangement.

Increasingly the tourist agencies are handling the business of private lettings, which is probably just as well. But occasionally women with free rooms still come down to meet the ferries, or accost tourists in the streets, even though the practice is supposed to be illegal. Many a past village quarrel was caused by the 'poaching' of tourists, who were thought to have committed themselves to another. Complaints, if necessary, and initial enquiries too, can always be made with the police.

Cell accommodation is occasionally available in monasteries.

(Opposite) *Faint echoes of Venice and its colonial rule attend an arrival in Levkas town from the mainland; the atmosphere of the capital is unique, and contrasts delightfully with the rest of the island (see page 161).*

Camping

Although the NTOG itself runs a number of campsites on the mainland, with reliable standards and reasonable services, it has none on the islands. Indeed there are fewer campsites on the islands, in relation to demand, than on the mainland; during the season their capacity is severely stretched. An island with several campsites may give no better chance of finding a place, but only shows the island is attractive to campers. NTOG is doing what it can to encourage the opening of more sites, but progress is slow. A particular difficulty seems to be the rather high specifications insisted on for new sites, which involve a capital outlay beyond the means of many islanders. On other islands the authorities do not wish to encourage campers, because of the poor image acquired by too many of that fraternity. Unofficial campsites, which open adventitiously during the season, can sometimes be found in olive groves, fields, or patches of land next to hotels and restaurants. Fees are likely to be about half those for licensed sites, but for fewer facilities. Particulars of functioning official campsites are listed under each island in Part 2. **Levkas** and **Zakynthos** are well provided with a range of sites; there are two good sites in **Kefallonia,** but none in **Ithaka.** The scope for free camping, the water situation, and availability of Camping Gas exchange bottles (expendable cartridges are widely stocked) are also discussed in Part 2.

It is a good idea to have an international camping carnet. Not only is this document a token of respectability, which can be deposited with management in lieu of a passport; but its modest cost can easily be recovered from the discounts widely available on campsite fees.

Camping outside campsites is supposed to be illegal in Greece, and notices to this effect are frequently seen. But large numbers of holiday-makers do arrive, either expecting to be able to camp, or prepared to do so in the event of cheap lodgings not being readily available. Police attitudes vary from island to island; but in general it would be contrary to Greek traditions of hospitality, besides damaging for the tourist trade, to turn campers away. In any case the small numbers of police are greatly overstretched during the season. Usually they confine themselves to going through the motions of moving campers on, from time to time: these token gestures become more vigorous only in response to complaints (about noise, smell or other nuisance) from local residents or resentful owners of hotels and campsites.

Otherwise the main preoccupation of the authorities is the fearful danger of forest fires, which can so easily be started by careless campers. The occurrence of such fires has increased greatly, its growth more or less in line with the increasing number of campers. Every summer television news programmes show scenes of forest fires raging out of control, in spite of the efforts of fire brigades — supported by relays of seaplanes, drenching the blaze with tons of seawater — to contain them. The ferocity and terror of these infernoes has to be experienced to be believed, whilst the dismal and totally wasteful consequences are to be seen in parts of most islands. Campers — and people who smoke — should bear this in mind at all times. Article 206 of Law 86/69 can be rigorously applied, stating as it does that "The punishment for lighting a fire in the forest, *for whatever purpose,* is at least two months in prison". This is one Greek law which it would be unwise to trifle with. (Drug smuggling would come into the same category.)

A part-time fisherman of Kariotes prepares his boat for a night's fishing in waters at the south end of the Levkas Channel.

SIX

Food, drink and entertainment

What to expect of Greek food

Few people would place Greek cooking very high in a league table of *haute cuisine*. And it is undeniable that general standards of Greek island cooking fall below those on the mainland. Further, the choice is more limited. At its best, Greek island food is fresh, tasty and satisfying. The problem is that during the summer, because kitchens are unbearably hot, and probably large numbers of hungry customers sit waiting to be served, standards fall below their best.

Of course these are generalisations. The Ionian islands have had the great advantage of a long tradition of good eating — which it must be said owes more to the Italian than the British influence! It is unfortunate that the individuality of the Ionian island cuisine today is much diluted, no doubt because of the regrettable reluctance of too many foreign tourists to try anything new. Undeniably it is quite difficult to find anymore those speciality dishes for which the islands used to be noted — the few exceptions are mentioned in Part 2. The homogenisation process continues, but — both Kefallonia and Zakynthos can nevertheless point to a number of restaurants, including hotel restaurants, as good as the best comparable establishments on the mainland. Levkas and Ithaka, if less sophisticated, also have their bright spots.

Most larger restaurants offer some choice of international dishes, in addition to Greek food. Smaller restaurants tend to specialise in fish *(psaria)* or meat *(skaras)* — both usually served grilled. Fish nowadays tends to be rather expensive, but looks even more so on menus, when the written price usually indicates price per kilo — so a single portion will cost only a fraction of that.

Many islanders themselves enjoy eating out, but not usually in those establishments along the waterfront and other places frequented by large numbers of tourists. Tucked away inside the town or out in the countryside are little places where they can enjoy traditional meals in a customary atmosphere. It's normal for their meals to be served warm, rather than hot — that's because housewives have had an understandable preference to do as much as possible of their cooking in the relative cool of the morning, and they warm it later as required.

Tavernas and restaurants

At the lowest end of the scale comes the humble *taverna,* comparable to the French *bistro* and Italian *trattoria* — a place where simple cooking can be enjoyed amid modest surroundings. The main difference between taverna and restaurant is that the latter opens at lunch-time as well as in the evening and probably provides a small selection of desserts, coffee and after dinner drinks. But thanks to some well known films, and abetted by tourist propaganda, the taverna image has been overlain with notions of music, dancing and mingling with the locals, in some romantic situation beside a starlit beach. Tourists therefore come to the islands eager to eat in tavernas — and so many restaurants have found it necessary to describe themselves as tavernas!

On the Ionian islands the *tavérna* actually originated as a simple drinking-house, along the lines of the English tavern of the same period. But as the islands became absorbed into the Greek nation, and especially since the arrival of tourism, the Ionian taverna has become much the same as anywhere else in Greece.

The Greeks are great nibblers of food in between meals, if need be straight out of some plastic packet. But long before Colonel Sanders made his mark on the West, they already had years of experience of convenience food. Most island towns have at least one *souvlaki* stall, probably opening in the late morning as well as the evening — even if in the more sophisticated islands you may find it disguised as a snack bar. The proper filling of the *souvlaki* is some chunks of grilled lamb, mixed with raw tomato, onion and spices, wrapped in a small pancake called *pitta.* Unfortunately rather ordinary bread rolls are often substituted for pitta and, what is more, sometimes not even toasted as they should be. A number on the price list — 1, 2 or 3 — indicates the number of skewers of meat included in the filling. Many variations on the *souvlaki,* including close approximations to hamburgers and hot dogs, can be found. Other popular convenience snacks include cheese pies *(tiropites)* and toasted sandwiches *(tost).* Increasingly too pizzerias are found, their product more in the French rather than Italian style.

Many establishments use a standardised menu, with a vast range of dishes printed on it. In fact only those with prices beside them are available (the two prices are with and without tax). In any case it's quite the done thing to go into the kitchen to see precisely what is on offer. It's usual to leave a 10 per cent tip, divided between the waiter and the boy who brought the bread and drinks. Restaurants sometimes have two price lists, the cheaper one being for dishes taken away. Whole sheep or goats, roasted on the spit, are sometimes sold in take-away portions, costed by weight.

Much nibbling also goes on in cafés (more correctly *kafeneions).* These are primarily in the business of serving drinks of all kinds: hot and cold, beers, wines and spirits. But so long do the Greeks have to wait for their evening meal that it is normal, even prudent, to nibble something with the aperitif. This is called *mezes* (singular) or *mezethes* (plural), and in the more traditional drinking places is probably included in the price of the drink: otherwise it can be ordered and paid for separately.

Two other typically Greek types of eating place are the *galaklopoleio,* specialising in milk products and sometimes honey, and the *zacharoplasteion,* which specialises in cakes and pastries. The former can be useful at breakfast, as an alternative to a taverna, whilst the latter is fine for a mid morning or afternoon snack, as well as the best place to come for your sweet course, after an evening meal at a taverna.

Drinks

Greek coffee is similar to Turkish — but better not order it as such! It is always served black in a *demi-tasse* with an accompanying glass of cold water. Never stir it, and beware of the considerable amount of sediment at the bottom. You choose your amount of sugar: without *skéto;* with a little sugar *médrio;* incredibly sweet *gleekó.*

Greek beer is good, another legacy from King Otho, who brought techniques, equipment and a skilled *braumeister* down from his native Bavaria. The oldest and best known brand has been *Fix,* but *Amstel* and *Henninger* are more often found in the bars today.

Wine is made in all the south Ionian islands, some of it very good indeed, especially in Kefallonia, where a large proportion is exported. Good examples can be found in all the islands. But much wine on sale in island shops comes over more cheaply from the mainland. Cheap Greek wines commonly prove rather disappointing, compared with a French *vin du pays* or Italian *vino di tavola:* too often they are blandly mass produced or, if local, have been crudely made. Much of the medium and dry white wines are at least slightly resinated. The Greeks prefer it that way — the habit is no more debased than smoking menthol cigarettes, however the purist may dislike it! As for the famous and controversial *retsina,* that is best thought of as in a class of its own.

Waterside café, looking across to the Meganisi ferry berth (just off picture, left). The local policeman is among the customers.

Red wines are not often resinated, but instead may well seem rather sweet to a foreign palate. A bottle with *demi-doux* on the label will probably be very sweet indeed. The few dryer red wines, on the other hand, are often quite pleasant. Also agreeable, especially for drinking late into the evening, are some sweet white wines, such as the celebrated wine of Samos — a favourite with Lord Byron, which today can be bought throughout Greece.

The native Greek spirits are brandy and ouzo. Both seem amazingly cheap, especially when bought direct from the barrel into your own empty bottle. Cheap brandy, though undeniably potent, may disappoint on account of its crude, sweet, perfumed and almost soapy flavour. Better qualities come mostly in the bottle, graded from three to seven stars — the higher the number the more mature (and expensive, of course). *Cambas* and *Metaxas* are reliable brands, found everywhere, whilst *Achaia Clauss* has its factory near Patras (see Chapter 14). The cheaper ouzo, on the other hand, often seems very good, especially when made locally. Ouzo is an aniseed-flavoured spirit, colourless when neat, which turns milky when water is added. Thus it is a close relative of *pastis* and similar drinks found throughout the Mediterranean. When served in a café, a large glass of water will invariably accompany it. They do not need to be drunk mixed. But if retribution by hangover is to be avoided, by one means or another a lot of water must be drunk.

There are several types of traditional Greek drinking place, from *kafeneion,* through *kafebar,* to *ouzerie.* It's very rare indeed to find a Greek woman in any of these, although foreign girls will be tolerated. But foreigners of both sexes may find the atmosphere too rigid and male-dominated to be congenial, and prefer instead the warmer ambience of a *pub.* Prices will be significantly higher because these places do little business outside the tourist season; but the owner — an educated Greek or expatriate — will be prepared to chat to you for hours, dispensing all the free local information you could ask for, often in an atmosphere of soft lights and taped music.

Drink (and food) price levels are all authorised by the tourist police, who take into account the facilities available before setting the prices. Thus the same beer bought for 50 drs in a café, may cost 100drs in a pub or 150drs at a discothque. The cheapest way to get round high drink prices is to buy a bottle of wine and share it.

For those returning from Greece by sea the two duty-free shops in the port of Patras offer a very good choice of wines and spirits at exceptionally competitive prices.

Entertainment

Nightclubs are found in the larger island capitals, in the big hotels, and occasionally elsewhere.

Most towns have a cinema, where the soundtrack is normally in the original language, with sub-titles in Greek. There are additional open-air cinemas in summer. The demand from younger holidaymakers ensures that discos are found on all the islands. They are usually situated on the outskirts of towns and villages, and since ownership and even location are prone to change from year to year, these are not for the most part listed specifically in Part 2. Not all discos make an admission charge, but where they do it will include the price of your first drink.

The traditional popular music of the Ionian islands is the *kantádes,* an Italianised kind of folk-song accompanied by string instruments such as guitars. Military bands were introduced by the British, and these continue to flourish. Imported *bouzouki* can be heard on most islands, sometimes played by live musicians in a restaurant or special club. The dancing that often spontaneously accompanies it is known as *syrtaki* (though there are other forms of dance); non-Greek onlookers may well be encouraged to join in as the evening wears on!

On the radio there are daily news programmes and weather forecasts in English. On weekdays there is also a daily news bulletin on television. This follows the 1800 evening news in Greek, on the Second Programme, and usually finishes with a brief weather forecast.

Sport and recreation

Caiques can be hired by the day or hour, for **fishing** or private excursions. Otherwise it may be possible to make arrangements to accompany a fishing caique. Pedalos, often for hire on the more popular beaches, can be made use of for limited fishing excursions.

Caique owners should be able to suggest favourable spots to find fish. They may even supply the gear. Alternatively some specialist shops do exist where fishing tackle can be bought or hired. Greek fishermen often dig their own bait from some sandy beach; but maggots are sometimes sold. Fish are less plentiful than they used to be, and now that Greece has joined the EEC Italian boats often come across in pursuit of the choicer species.

Breathing apparatus can sometimes be hired for underwater **swimming.** Its use is restricted by law to designated areas, in order to prevent the plundering of antiquities, and only hand-operated spears should be used.

Waterskiing, windsurfing, parascending, sailing and **boating** are available on most of the islands, but other sports are not yet much developed. There are two public **tennis** courts in Zakynthos town, run by the NTOG; elsewhere those belonging to the big hotels are usually available for hire to non-residents, together with equipment. Donkeys, mules or horses can sometimes be hired for **riding** excursions. There are no **golf** courses as yet. **Bicycles** can be hired in almost all the tourist areas.

Shooting takes place on all the islands, but only Greeks and resident foreigners are permitted to apply for the shooting licences, which are obligatory except perhaps on the Kefallonia game farm.

View back to the village from the breakwater. Even a yachtsman from the USA has been drawn here, by the magic of Ithaka and the marvellous sailing conditions that exist in its offshore waters.

Basket making (with the 'Kalamos' reeds) a cottage industry still alive and well in a back street of Argostoli.

SEVEN

Shopping

The cost of living on an island — any island — is almost bound to be greater than on the mainland, since so many of the goods consumed (and most of the tourist goods) are nowadays brought in from outside, and so must bear the quite considerable cost of sea transport. Whilst fruit and vegetables are grown on the islands, much of it is for private consumption. The average quality of fresh produce is unremarkable, especially by the time it has reached the islands, and rarely compares with Italy or the South of France. Choice is also limited — lettuce, for example, can be hard to find. Once again Levkas, being virtually part of the mainland, is largely an exception to this generalisation.

The transport factor may occasionally work to the tourist's advantage, if an island's own products are exported in quantity. Thus honey and wine in Kefallonia, lace and embroidery in Levkas, and perfume in Zakynthos, cost less in island shops than on the mainland.

Greek produced goods as a whole seem quite reasonably priced, whilst imports of all sorts are more expensive — though some convergence can be expected as 1992 approaches. Cigarettes are an example, with local brands costing but a fraction of imports. The tobacco, mostly grown in the north of the country, is usually good, but tightness of packing and effectiveness of the filter may seem inferior. A degree of bargaining over the more expensive tourist goods is usually in order. Ceramics, leather, cheesecloth dresses, silver jewellery, sponges and worry beads *(komboloi)* are usually good value — these products are distributed nationally.

There are few things that cost sufficiently more in Greece to make it worth bringing them out from home. Photographic film may be an exception, whilst black and white film is often impossible to find on the islands. If you plan to be self-catering, beef stock cubes, coffee whitener and bran fibre are about the only things of any consequence you'll probably not find in an island supermarket.

Shop opening hours

These are controlled by law. Food shops, for example, are supposed to stay closed for three evenings of the week as well as all day on Sunday, regulations that are observed in traditional places. But in most holiday areas they are not; of course there is a period of closing in the middle of the day but after that shops stay open as long as the owner thinks there is a chance of doing business.

Street kiosks *(periptero)* which also open for an amazingly long period, often without lunch break, are found in the towns. They sell a wide range of small items, most obviously books and magazines, postcards and cigarettes. Many of them keep a telephone with meter for public use (see below).

Books and newspapers

Most islands have shops where English language books can be bought. This usually takes the form of a display rack containing a standard selection of popular paperbacks. Where there are lots of tourists the choice improves. Prices are at least 50 per cent above UK prices.

The more popular tourist areas have shops where used foreign language books can be exchanged. You choose between paying a small fee per book exchanged, or taking away half the number of books brought in, without payment.

UK daily and Sunday papers arrive regularly in the islands, usually the day after printing. A locally produced alternative is the *Athens News.*

Currency and banks

Greek currency is denominated in drachmae. Notes of 1000, 500, 100 and 50 drachmae, and coins of 50, 20, 10, 5, and 1 drachmae, are in common use. A new 5000dr note has been introduced, but is often difficult to get changed. The old ½dr coin is no longer legal tender, whilst the 50dr note is on the way out. In theory the drachma divides into 100 lepta, but this is of little practical consequence. Small change is sometimes in short supply.

The value of the Greek currency has been falling in recent years, so offsetting for tourists from 'hard currency' countries much of the effects of inflation from which the Greek people themselves suffer. In early 1989 the exchange rate against sterling was 270drs = 1 (i.e. each drachma was worth less than a UK halfpenny), although tourists get a somewhat less favourable rate in Greece itself than in the UK.

There is no limit to the amount of foreign currency permitted to be brought into Greece. Large amounts can also be taken out again, provided they were properly declared on entry. But the amount of local currency permitted to be brought in or out is closely controlled, though the limit has recently been increased from 3,000drs to an altogether more practical 25,000drs per person.

The main islands have branches of national banks — usually the National Bank of Greece and the Commercial Bank of Greece — as well as one or two regional banks such as the Ionian and Popular, which can handle any transaction in which the tourist might be interested. Tourist areas without a proper bank will have some arrangement, usually organised by a travel agent or prominent shopkeeper in association with one of the national banks, to permit foreign currency and travellers cheques (including Eurocheques denominated in drachmae) to be changed. Cheques drawn on the UK National Giro can be changed for drachmae at any Greek post office. Don't forget you need to produce your passport whenever changing a cheque.

Standard banking hours are from about 8am to 2pm Mondays to Fridays. During the season some banks in island capitals may open for a couple of hours later in the afternoon. Saturday opening can be encountered in Athens and other large towns on the mainland (for Patras see Chapter 3). Banks at road frontiers and Athens airport are also open on Sundays. Outside banking hours the larger hotels usually change money, even for non-residents — but naturally at a less favourable rate. On Monday mornings long queues of newly arrived tourists usually form outside the banks, and with the increasing popularity of the giro with continental tourists, at post offices too.

If you plan to stay longer than six months in Greece, save the pink exchange slips, as you will need them when applying for your visa.

Post offices

Poste restante mail seems to be scrupulously handled by island post offices *(taxydromeion,* the x pronounced as h). It will be held for at least the statutory four weeks, for collection against identification (passport), before eventually being returned to sender. Naturally, some difficulties can occur over deciphering handwriting in the Latin alphabet. Whilst letters are filed alphabetically, they may well be found under a forename or title even Mr, Mrs or Esq. Most officials will cooperate if politely asked to have another look.

Postage stamps are on sale in post offices. But it may be more convenient to use a shop or kiosk — mostly stamps are kept wherever postcards are sold. Such establishments are legally entitled to charge 10 per cent over and above the face value of the stamps.

Telephones

Telephone kiosks have either blue or orange bands at the top of their sides. The blue ones are for domestic calls, and use 10dr coins. Only the relatively few telephone kiosks with an orange box can be used for international calls; these take 10, 20 and 50dr coins. All these boxes are prone to faults — though rarely through vandalism — and you can get cut off if you fail to spot the tiny dim red light that's supposed to give warning. Thus it's often simpler to use a metered phone in an hotel, restaurant or *periptero.* In addition each town has an OTE (pronounced oh tay) office with booths containing metered telephones. The counter clerk will allocate you a booth and take your money on completion — which in any case will be less than you would have paid to make the same call from elsewhere. Telephone offices also handle telegrams, but it would normally be cheaper to phone.

The international prefix for the UK from Greece is 0044, followed by the UK STD code, less any initial 0.

EIGHT

Your health and comfort

Medical care

Doctors and chemists entirely adequate to the needs of tourism are found in all the islands. In the Ionian they are well-accustomed to treating foreigners, and a number of them speak one or more foreign languages — local information offices, tourist police and tour operators' representatives can give you information about this. Chemists are able to dispense many drugs which would be on prescription in the UK, and many of them are more experienced in treating common ailments than the younger doctors. All the islands have at least one hospital, where many conditions can be satisfactorily dealt with; the more difficult cases can, if necessary, quite easily be transferred to Patras or even Athens.

Doctors come regularly to the villages to hold surgeries. The buildings concerned are usually central and self-evident, with a notice giving the hours of attendance. They are often staffed by young 'barefoot doctors', doing their initial post-qualification period. Unless this is served in a rural area, salaries paid to these young doctors are very low indeed.

In theory, possession of form E.111 (see DHSS leaflet SA 30) entitles you to medical treatment at token cost. That should even include evacuation to the mainland if necessary. (Military helicopters are often used in emergency, occasionally even a passing submarine has been pressed into service.) In practice, for reasons that include the difficulty of completing the required paperwork, holidaymakers may well have to settle for private treatment. Insurance is compulsory with most packaged tours, and the independent traveller would be foolish to come out without such cover. Nevertheless the cost of private consultations and prescriptions is less than in northern Europe — currently a consultation costs about the equivalent of £5 sterling.

No vaccination certificates are required for entry into Greece from the UK, but the DHSS does recommend protection against typhoid. A booster injection would be needed three years after any previous vaccination.

Burns and bites

Care needs to be taken when starting sunbathing, because cooling winds can disguise the real heat of the sun — half an hour's exposure may well be enough for the first time. Mosquitoes can be a great hazard in some parts of most of the islands, as they are throughout much of the Mediterranean. Some hotels and campsites carry out successful preventative programmes in their own vicinities, but the extent of the nuisance is impossible to predict. Fortunately products to kill or repell mosquitoes and to sooth stings can be bought virtually everywhere — as also can creams and lotions for use before and after sunbathing — and these are usually cheaper than at home.

Water

Water supply is not usually a problem in the Ionian islands, except in Ithaka and parts of Kefallonia (see Part 2). Town drinking water is bacteriologically safe, but may well be strongly mineralised, so many people buy the excellent bottled water that is widely and cheaply available. Comments on the water supply situation on each island are found in Part 2 under the camping section.

Toilets

Public conveniences are seen less often than at home, though the situation is less acute than in some Aegean islands. The vicinity of any bus station or food market will usually be fruitful. It is also normally acceptable to make use of facilities in hotels or bars. You don't even have to be a customer, but they prefer it if you are! Ask for the *toe alletta*.

Toilets are often of the 'hole in the ground' type; the knack of using them is soon acquired, and they are easier to keep clean with a hose-pipe. Be careful not to lose the contents of your pocket down the hole! The fastidious should bring their own toilet paper, just in case. You might also like to 'be prepared' with one of those 'universal' type of basin plugs in your pocket.

Electricity

The 220v AC supply, compatible with UK domestic appliances, is now almost universal in Greece. Power sockets are usually for plugs of the German type — two pins with double earthing strap. Double-earthed travel appliances can safely be connected via a continental two-pin adaptor. Light bulbs use screw type sockets.

A little-frequented beach, shingle with a scattering of sand, near Piso Aetos.

NINE

About the South Ionian Islands

Ever since the time of the Norman conquests, European powers with imperial or commercial ambitions towards the East have recognised the great value of the Ionian islands as defensible staging posts along this primary line of communication. It usually happened that most of the group would find itself under the dominion of a single power; a power, moreover, who had neither the ambition nor need to control the adjoining mainland. And so administrative and commercial networks were created more to link the islands one to another rather than to the Greek mainland, as was more generally the case elsewhere. Between the eleventh and mid-nineteenth centuries the islands were undoubtedly deprived to some extent of their ethnic heritage; but in return they received the tangible benefit of exposure to the more advanced culture and technology of the occupying power. That was certainly the case for Kefallonia, Ithaka and Zakynthos; Levkas, for most practical purposes a part of the mainland, must be partly excepted — whilst the effects of a different set of influences there continue to be apparent.

In colonial times the Ionian islands were sometimes known as the Eptanisos, from their seven principal members: Corfu, Paxos and Kythira are not the subject of this book; of the other four, Kefallonia, Levkas and Zakynthos are today independent administrative districts each governed by a 'nomarch', whilst Ithaka is one of four 'eparchies' comprising the 'nome' of Kefallonia.

By the time of their return to Greece in 1864 most of the islands were culturally and economically well in advance of other Greek islands, and indeed of much of the mainland. Their new situation on the periphery of the Greek nation, and the abrupt removal of the protective economic umbrella previously enjoyed, did much to reduce their advantage — as again more recently did damage by earthquake. As this has been made good, so their touristic assets and attractions have once more put fresh impetus behind the development and prosperity of the Ionian islands, which has proved sufficient to halt and possibly even reverse the century-old decline in the population.

Plant life

The successful development of plant life depends on climate — temperature and rainfall profiles, wind effects — and the properties of the soil. In general the Ionian islands provide a more fortunate combination of these than does the Aegean, an ampler rainfall being the most important factor. Taking as an example an admittedly extreme comparision between Zakynthos and Mykonos — two islands of almost equal latitude — the former enjoys four times as much rainfall; and even more important, the period of very high soil-moisture deficit in summer is much less protracted. Soil too tends to be more fertile and deeper in the Ionian, and nature's provision can more conveniently be extended by terracing. And although the once well-covered mountains have suffered from timber-cutting, forest fires and goats, significant stands of natural woodland remain. From these easier circumstances both cultivated and natural flora have benefited.

Among the trees introduced into the islands is the eucalyptus (mainly the Tasmanian blue gum), which has become self-propagating. In addition to its useful timber and an oil extracted from its leaves, it was believed to help combat malaria — one of several reasons the peasants were reluctant to move away from their mountain villages — by restricting the breeding of mosquitos. Poplars too are planted for their timber, and planes grow well where the drainage is to their liking — some Levkadian villages have spectacular examples shading their fountains. Other common deciduous trees are various oaks, and the hop-hornbeam with its conspicuous yellow catkins. Kefallonia and Zakynthos still have substantial areas of pine, whilst stands of Italian cypress are found to some extent in all the islands. Uncultivated hillsides are often covered in healthy evergreen *maquis* scrub, among which small trees such as holly oak, juniper, strawberry tree and the red-berried mastic bring colourful relief to a carpeting of smaller and often-aromatic plants.

Spring is, of course, the time to enjoy the most spectacular display of wild flowers. Drifts of purple and yellow, blue, pink and white appear on all the islands, from spurge and broom, anemone and gladiolus, orchid, almond, asphodel and many others. In Zakynthos and parts of Levkas the whole landscape seems to explode into a fantasy of colour and perfume. The rains of autumn bring forth a secondary display.

Agriculture

In the past the occupying power often willed the means to stimulate agriculture, by means of planting subsidies and guaranteed crop prices — a benefit as helpful in the long run to the subjects as to their rulers. As a result parts of all the islands, especially Zakynthos and Levkas, are covered by small forests of long-living olive trees. Once established these continue to yield at least moderate crops of fruit and, almost as important, firewood, at little further expense; whereas grubbing the trees and clearing the land would call for substantial new investment. Like considerations also apply to

Late September sunshine on the outskirts of Argassi. A long line of assorted tractor-drawn trucks waits for the weighing and sampling of the grapes at the wine factory gate, before unloading inside.

grapes, whether planted originally for wine or currants. However there are economic consequences. For well over a decade, mountains of butter (which competes with oil for culinary use) and lakes of surplus wine have been clogging the mechanisms of the EEC agricultural policy. So whilst oil and wine are in principle ideal for trading, occupying but a small volume in relation to their value, prices are currently very low. This means that the 'terms of trade' against imported motor cars, household appliances and high technology are generally unfavourable for Greece.

It was not always so. In classical times the joys of wine were as much appreciated as today, and chieftains expected to provide it for their loyal supporters. Olives were even more valuable then than now, providing an important element in diet, a substitute for soap, and the sole easily available fuel for lamps. Skilful husbandry could produce surplus oil and wine for export, permitting quantities of grain and other useful commodities to be got in return. That was one of the factors making it possible in ancient times for small islands to support much larger populations than in later periods. But as knowledge of production techniques spread into Italy and Asia Minor, the commercial advantage was lost; in the absence of any external economic stimulus, populations could only diminish.

Animal life

A goodly number of bird species have been able to find conditions to suit them among the diversity of environments on offer. Inland mountain sanctuaries favour hawks, buzzards, ravens and even a few eagles; at lower levels scrub merges into coniferous and deciduous woodland, both interspersed with open glades, whilst cultivated fields and terraces surround the many small centres of human habitation — all of which provide specialised niches for finches, wheatears, warblers and others. Around the coastline precipitous cliffs give shelter to larger sea birds such as gulls, cormorants, and even an occasional osprey or sea eagle. Low-lying shores with marshes, swamps, salt-pans and sea-lakes furnish further rich variety for waders and their kind. Keen bird watchers most certainly have an enviable array of habitats within which to deploy their binoculars. And even casual amateurs are quite likely to get a chance sighting of one of those black-tipped cinnamon head-crests that so unmistakably distinguishes the hoopoe, even if glimpses of the equally spectacular golden oriole and the blue rock thrush are more likely to elude unpremeditated encounter.

The benefactions of butterflies, bees and dragonflies must be balanced against the discomforts of flies, midges, mosquitos and even scorpions, when evaluating the swings and roundabouts of the insect world.

Land animals are present in lesser array, due mainly to the activities, past and present, of man the hunter. But smaller creatures unfit for the pot remain in plenty to provide diversion to any country walk. Lizards pop up from behind stones, tortoises amble beside the footpaths, frogs call to one another from muddy pools, and snakes — mostly harmless — slither through the undergrowth.

Geology

The islands themselves are the sunken peaks of mountains once linked to mainland ranges, evidence that this is an area of exciting geological turbulence. The feature of most concern to visitors is its situation at the margins of tectonic plates — the fault lines along which earthquakes take place. The people have had to adapt themselves to this phenomenon from the very first. Public buildings, if they were to last, needed to be squat and unpretentious, whilst private homes had to protect their occupants from more than just the three elements of air, fire and water. Over the millennia the population has learned to accept the impermanence of structures, water supplies, and other such normally-fixed utilities, and to contrive improvisations and unconventional solutions to cope with the unstable conditions.

Whilst archeologists struggle to impose order on their jumble of fragmentary evidence from the past, and historians work with geographers to unravel the economic and social changes resulting from variations in shore levels, what ordinary visitors will want to know is: how safe is it to come out here for a holiday? Fortunately our risk is, in objective terms, pretty minute. Really severe earthquakes such as that of 1953 are very rare, perhaps once every four or five hundred years. The few modern buildings constructed by 1953 suffered little more than minor damage; and all subsequent buildings have been designed to survive at least as destructive upheavals. We are probably under greater risk as we travel here in our aeroplane, or drive in our car to the airport, or even whilst cooking a meal in our own kitchen. Life itself can be considered as just one great series of risk probabilities; perhaps the best philosophy is simply to relax and enjoy it?

Beaches

The general standard of beaches in the Ionian islands is high, whilst the very best beaches on Kefallonia, Levkas and Zakynthos can hold comparison with any in the Mediterranean. The more popular ones have attention drawn to them in the individual island chapters in Part 2. Most of these enjoy at least the services of a drinks seller during the season, whilst many have a seasonal taverna *(kéndron)* near at hand; waterskiing, windsurfing, sailing and boating are often to be found, when some sort of instruction is usually available.

Greek law officially forbids nudity, which most Greek island people find genuinely offensive. Where callous individuals peel off completely on their town beaches, mothers may feel obliged to take an alternative route home with their school children. To prevent such public nuisance, police have been known to don swimming trunks and look for naturists, before returning in uniform to make their arrests. In fact those islands frequented by foreign tourists probably have at least one isolated beach set aside where nudism/naturism is unofficially tolerated. As for toplessness, it is nowadays more or less acceptable on any isolated beach: the higher the proportion of foreigners to Greeks, the more it occurs.

Sandy beaches seem preferred by most holidaymakers. But rocky beaches have their advantages too, especially for snorkelling in the clearer water. Those without flippers would be wise to wear plastic beach-shoes; rocks can become very slippery, whilst prickly sea-urchins may lie concealed below. There is a law restricting the use of underwater breathing apparatus — both for swimming and fishing — to certain designated areas, which was introduced to prevent plundering of underwater antiquities by would-be treasure hunters. In practice nobody is likely to be prevented from using this gear around tourist beaches.

Jelly fish seem to be on the increase everywhere these days. Travelling around in small shoals, they come and go unpredictably since, though chiefly driven by wind and current, they can also propel themselves. They come in a wide range of sizes and colours, the transparent ones being most difficult to spot, whilst the pale brown ones have the worst sting. This is certainly painful for a few hours, but an anti-allergic jelly, as used for insect bites, may help.

Ammonia is another panacea, which you can buy in a sachet at the pharmacy; even closer to hand, it's readily available in the form of urine!

It is a traditional Greek custom to take the first bathe of the year on Ascension Day, which falls six weeks after Easter. But for us northerners the sea should not seem too cold even at Easter.

Road systems

The four main islands covered by this book have well-developed road networks, by comparison with the Greek island average. All main roads are tarmac, and many have been re-aligned in the recent past; whilst a higher proportion of the minor roads are hard-surfaced than elsewhere. Standards of maintenance vary; whereas those on Ithaka and Levkas are good, in parts of the other two islands you are only too likely to encounter moped riders more pre-occupied with avoiding pot-holes than attending to the presence of other road-users.

The extent of the main network is indicated on each island map, although naturally additions continue. There are also unsurfaced motor tracks, sometimes recently bulldozed, and wide enough for lorry traffic. Some of them are an essential part of the island road network, awaiting only funds to permit a covering of tarmac. Then there are tracks to meet the needs of forest management, agriculture, quarrying, or the military. Their condition varies widely, depending on terrain, recent weather and time elapsed since they were last graded. Private cars can often travel considerable distances along them, without discomfort; but sometimes at critical points they become impassable. Traditional mule tracks continue to exist, but in the Ionian these tend to be of local interest only.

It is certainly true that holidaymakers can manage quite well without their own car. All the islands have buses and plenty of taxis, even if the bus service in Ithaka is rather nominal. Cars, motorbikes, mopeds and bicycles can be hired on all the islands (see Chapters 12 and 13 for typical rates). But if a car has already been brought to Greece, it will normally be convenient to continue to have the use of it on the island, particularly as the car-ferry services are so satisfactory.

Petrol and diesel fuel are freely available in most parts of the islands — the few deficiencies in local distribution are mentioned in Part 2 under individual islands. Proficient repair of routine vehicle defects can be made at all the towns.

Motorbike and moped rental

Motorbikes, or more usually mopeds, are readily available in most of the tourist areas, and many of us will be tempted to hire one, regardless of our recent riding experience. Most hire bikes will have seen better days, whilst tell-tale signs of rough treatment can be hidden easily enough under a coat of paint. Some important points to remember when hiring are:

● Make sure it works. Take it for a test run, which will also ensure you can handle it!

● Negotiate the price, especially if hiring for more than a day. Does this include petrol? What insurance cover is included?

● Make a note of the agency 'phone number in case of breakdown. They have their own breakdown trucks which don't sit idle for long!

● Don't be ashamed to ask for a crash helmet. These are not yet compulsory in Greece, and they won't do a thing to enhance your sporting image. But they cost no extra, and may prove to be your salvation: there are so many 'holiday drivers' around in the summer that even if *you* know what you are doing, you may fall foul of someone else who doesn't. Accidents happen every day, even if most of those involved get away with cuts and bruises.

● Make a firm arrangement about the time you will return the bike. Your hire may be 'for the day', but if you return it after 1900 you'll find yourself unpopular with the employee who has had to work late for you. If you want to keep it until first thing next morning, make that clear.

● Don't forget they drive on the right hand side in Greece!

● If roads are pot-holed, look for a bike with large wheels. If you want to go up into the mountains, or down steep tracks to get to beaches far below, a powerful motor is essential.

● Resist the temptation to take corners at speed.

If the engine stops functioning, check first that there is still petrol *(vin ze nee)* in the tank. Otherwise the problem probably lies with the ignition. Is the cable firmly attached to the sparking plug? Or, indeed, is the sparking plug still in place?

Remember it is against the law to drive motorised bikes through towns during the siesta (i.e. from 1300 to 1700), or to make other loud noises.

Time and distance

It's not wise to rely too closely on any estimates you may be given for time or distance. Local people do not think of journeys in simple terms of kilometres or minutes; in any case, for reasons of courtesy, they hold it more important to please you with optimism rather than disappoint you with inconvenient reality. For similar reasons commercial signposts sometimes understate distances to campsites and other attractions.

Beware too that *p.m.* in Greek, *prin mesimeri,* is before noon; *m.m., meta mesimeri,* is after noon.

Greek time is basically *two* hours ahead of Greenwich Mean Time. Greece also has a summer time (making it *three* hours ahead of GMT) but the dates may vary a little from British Summer Time, though in general the time difference remains the same.

Maps and walking excursions

Locally produced maps can be bought on the four principal islands. These are useful for making excursions, despite the quite substantial errors they often contain. New developments are often incorrectly incorporated, whilst tracks that disappeared years ago may still be retained.

The Clyde leisure map of the Ionian islands shows the relationship between the islands and the mainland admirably — though naturally the detail for individual islands is limited. Invaluable for the purposes of yachtsmen, and even some land-lubbers, is British Admiralty Chart 203 — Antipaxos to Cape Glarenza.

Some suggestions for walking excursions have been given in Part 2. Where mule tracks are involved a stout pair of walking shoes is advisable. When a time is given, this is for the single journey, by an averagely fit adult walking steadily. There would be wide differences for an experienced hiker or a family party.

Greek public holidays

01 Jan	New Year's Day and the Feast of St Basil.
06 Jan	Epiphany — and the Blessing of the Waters.
Feb	*Kathara Deftera* ('Clean Monday') — the first day of (Orthodox) Lent. Carnival celebrations reach their peak on this day and during the previous weekend.
25 Mar	Independance Day — anniversary of the initial pro- clamation of uprising in the Peloponnese in 1821, by Metropolitan Germanos of Patras.
Mar/Apr	(Orthodox) Good Friday — Holy Saturday — Easter Sunday.
01 May	International Labour Day — and/or Flower Festivals.
15 Aug	Assumption of the Virgin Mary.
28 Oct	*Okhi* Day — anniversary of the refusal by prime minister Metaxas to accept an ultimatum demanding passage of the Italian forces through Greece in 1940.
25 Dec	Christmas Day.
26 Dec	St Stephen's Day.

The anniversary of their union with Greece is widely celebrated in the Ionian islands on 21 May; but it is no longer a national holiday, any more than is 21 April, which used to commemorate the Colonels' revolution of 1967. Local holidays feature in Part 2 under individual island chapters.

History

One point of possible confusion needs to be explained, namely the apparent sameness in English of the 'Ionian' of the Ionian Islands and that of Ionia, the Greek-colonised coastal part of Asia Minor. Although the former usage is in fact quite modern, dating from the brief period of Russian interest during the French Revolution, the Ionian Sea had been known as such since the sixth century BC, and took its name, so Aeschylus tells us, from the nymph Io. The other Ionia — taken from the hero Ion — is spelt in Greek with the different (and longer) 'o'.

This section outlines a framework of key dates from Greek history affecting the Ionian islands — although it must be borne in mind that only after about 600 BC do the dates begin to become precise. It is interspersed with a rather more extended treatment of certain historical episodes, the material affects of which can still be noticed in the islands today.

6500 BC Approximate date when the first farmer settlers crossed the Bosphorus to arrive in Europe. There is plenty of fertile land for all comers, with no need for fortifications or weapons. Primitive boats already existed, so probably before long some settlers cross to the nearer and more fertile islands — perhaps even earlier, since some sites where flint tools were made on Kefallonia and Zakynthos have been dated as probably not later than 6000 BC.

2800 BC End of the Neolithic Age. Beginning of the Bronze Age.

2650 BC Beginning of the Minoan civilisation in Crete, where the skills of metalwork and pottery develop to great heights. Much trade, especially with Egypt. A time of great prosperity, with Minoan fleets keeping the peace of the eastern Mediterranean — though the Minoans themselves probably never maintained any settlements on the Ionian islands.

2000 BC Arrival and subsequent diffusion of the first Greek-speaking Indo-Europeans on the mainland.

1450 BC Minoan civilisation falls, because of disruption to trade, raiders from outside, and natural disasters. At about the same time the Greek-speaking kingdom based on Mycenae begins to dominate the Peloponnese, and then the Ionian islands beyond. Mycenaean ships ply the seas as pirates and traders.

C. 1200 BC The Trojan War. Agamemnon, King of Mycenae, leads an expedition against Troy, which traditionally fell to him in 1183 BC. Local rulers were obliged to supply their liege-lord with contingents of ships and soldiers, and some of them would have come from the Ionian islands. The Homeric view of this long war, and the return of Odysseus (Ulysses) to his homeland is discussed in Chapter 11 (under Homer's Ithaka). But whereas Homer considered the *casus belli* to have been the abduction of Helen, wife of Mycenaean chieftain Menelaus, by Trojan Prince Paris, in reality it was probably more to do with restrictions on trade, which had prevented Mycenaean access to profitable opportunities beyond the Dardanelles.

1100 BC End of the Bronze Age, Beginning of the Iron Age. Ownership of affective arms has hitherto been limited to the few could afford bronze. Now cheap weapons can be had by all. The Dorians, last Greek-speaking tribe to reach Greece, may already have mastered smelting techniques before their arrival, which now deals the final blow to aristocratic Mycenae, already weakened by over-indulgence in warfare. Local rulers in the Ionian islands and elsewhere are forced to take refuge in safer parts, especially near the Aegean mainland of Asia (thus for example Same in Kefallonia may have been the founder of Samos in the eastern Aegean).

C. 800 BC Homer, possibly a native of Chios, puts into writing, in his twin epic poems the *Iliad* and *Odyssey,* the old tales of gods and heroes in Mycenaean Times.

766 BC Ancient computed date for the first Olympic Games contest.

700-500 BC The Archaic Period. A great flowering of city states, to which the Ionian islands are somewhat peripheral. Experiments with political systems evolve into the essentials of Greek civilisation. As land becomes insufficient for increasing populations, a wave of colonisation sweeps out through the Ionian islands into Italy (Magna Graecia) and elsewhere. Power polarises between Athens and Sparta.

500-478 BC The Persian Wars. Greek and Persian expansionism interlock in conflict. This has little effect on the distant Ionian islands, although Levkas sent three ships to fight at the battle of Salamis (480).

478-431 BC The great age of Hellenism. Triumphant Athens assumes leadership in all things. Persians expelled from the Aegean, and piracy cleaned up yet again. Athens establishes naval bases in the Ionian islands, to support its continuing struggle against Sparta.

431-404 BC The Peloponnesian War. Sparta takes the lead to topple Athens. A disastrous defeat in far off Syracuse marks the beginning of the end for Athens. Subsequent struggles between Sparta and its former allies weaken them all.

359-200 BC The rise of Macedon, under Philip II and subsequently Alexander the Great, has little effect in the Ionian islands.

202 BC Rome, following its defeat of Carthage, declares war against Phillip V of Macedon in 200 BC. Levkas is taken in 197, Zakynthos in 191 and Kefallonia and Ithaka in 188.

146 BC The sack of Corinth. All Greece now forms part of the Roman province of Macedonia.

31 BC Fleet of Octavian defeats that of Anthony and Cleopatra near Preveza, at the Battle of Actium.

295 AD Finding his empire too large, and with too many problems to be ruled by one man from a single centre, Diocletian divides it into Western and Eastern parts. The first Christian emperor, Constantine (died 337 BC), builds a defensible capital for his Eastern Empire — to which the Ionian islands belong — on the site of the former Greek Byzantium, and calls it Constantinople. Athens sinks to the level of a minor provincial city, whereas Salonica (Thessaloniki) becomes second city of the Empire.

381 AD The Second Ecumenical Council grants the Bishop of Constantinople jurisdiction over the Church in Asia Minor and the Balkans — thus legitimising the future Greek Orthodox Church.

393 AD The Olympic Games are suppressed, nudity being offensive to the now Christian Byzantines.

Over the centuries Byzantine confronts successive invasions by Goths, Huns, Vandals, Slavs, Arabs and Bulgars, with varying degrees of success.

890 AD The Byzantine emperor Leo the Philosopher (886-911) forms all seven Ionian islands into one province with Kefallonia its capital, under which status they continue to belong to the Eastern Empire during and after the disintegration of Italy.

The Normans Their formal arrival on the main European scene came in 911, when Rollo, leader of a band of Viking sea-raiders, was persuaded to abandon his longboat invasion up the Seine by an offer of 'danegeld' from the French King Charles the Simple, in the form of the Dukedom of Normandy. By the end of the century their prolific descendants, though fully assimilated as Christian Frenchmen, continued to retain their appetite for travel and conquest. A band of forty such Normans, returning from a visit to the Holy Land in 1016, was persuaded that the south of Italy might be ripe for plunder — such was the weakness and oppression of Byzantine rule there, and the hatred of its subjects against taxation, compulsory military service and an alien (Orthodox) religion. The following year they returned, their numbers swollen by many of their knightly friends from Normandy, together with less reputable adventurers and hangers-on who joined them on the way. So superior was their fighting spirit, and so divided the local and regional rulers, that when eventually they drove out the Byzantines in 1071 they had been able to usurp for themselves control of virtually all south Italy including Sicily. One of their greatest leaders, Robert Guiscard (the Cunning), sixth son of an obscure and impoverished knight, ruled much of the mainland; and he saw an opportunity to put his proven but temporarily unoccupied fighting forces to the task of taking over the rest of the once mighty Byzantine empire, now sinking swiftly towards chaos. Near Durazzo in 1081 he was able to defeat an army under the Emperor Alexius I himself. Local populations offered him no further resistance, whilst his forces were even swelled by Byzantine desertions. But the need for Guiscard to return to deal with trouble in Italy was followed by an epidemic of typhoid which killed five hundred of his knights — and on his arrival in Kefallonia to resume command he too caught the fever and died in 1085. Subsequent attacks against the Empire were launched from Norman Sicily in the twelfth century — and their brief period of rule after 1182 in Kefallonia, Zakynthos and Ithaka was regarded as a great improvement over the Byzantine. But the Norman threat diminished greatly after 1194, when succession passed to the Holy Roman Emperors — usually perforce more preoccupied with problems in central Europe than southern Italy.

A wayside chapel in the south of Kefallonia, now derelict and abandoned following earthquake damage.

The Venetians The origins of Venice are even earlier than the Normans, having been founded by prosperous Roman citizens forced to flee during the Gothic invasion under Alaric in 402. They chose a remote and inaccessible stretch of coastal marshland for their refuge, where they built rudimentary communities on various low-lying islands. In 466 these agreed to amalgamate in self-government, and within a hundred years they were trading with many of the coastal towns in north and central Italy. This sea-borne exchange of salt, preserved fish and game for the many products they lacked was the beginning of their commercial empire, and of their navy too.

Situated as they were at the margin of the Byzantine empire, to which they were nominally subject, they found themselves able to play off the Emperor and his representatives against the 'barbarian' rulers of Italy. By the eleventh century they were so strong that the Emperor had several times to beg their help to keep the Norman threat at bay — help but sparingly given, in order to gain generous trading concessions in return, which further increased their strength. Venice was little involved in the First Crusade of 1096, when knights from various west European countries fought the Saracens in the Holy Land, their unexpected success resulting in several of them becoming petty rulers in the Levant — the beginning of the 'Frankish Territories' (the Byzantines used to call all Latin-speaking Christians Franks). But the Venetian power continued to increase, so by 1155 Byzantium was compelled to grant important trading concessions to the Genoese, in an attempt to counterbalance the Venetian advantage.

In 1204 Venice was able to benefit dramatically from its unique ability to undertake the sea transport of forces raised to fight the Fourth Crusade. An excuse was found to divert its intended destination from Egypt to Constantinople, which Christian city was captured and disgracefully plundered. Venice further emerged with the Ionian islands and much other Byzantine territory as its formal share of the booty. At this time the central state apparatus of Venice was insufficient directly to govern these, so they were leased to individual Venetian families — in the case of Kefallonia, Ithaka and Zakynthos to the Orsinis. Levkas continued for the moment under Greek rule, by a cousin of the deposed Emperor who called himself Despot of Epirus. In the fifteenth century all four islands came into the hands of the Tocco family.

In 1453 Constantinople fell to the Ottoman Turks, whose subsequent advance soon expelled the Franks from the Greek mainland. This now allowed Venice to reclaim sovereignty over islands (except at first Levkas). But between 1463 and 1718 Venice was to fight no fewer than seven wars against the Ottomans, which progressively drained it of its wealth and power. The fighting ebbed and flowed up and down the Ionian — during it Levkas, for example, changed hands no fewer than five times — even though the islands were not themselves central to the struggle, and indeed benefited much from their increasing importance to Venice. But as both Venice and the Ottomans bled fatally so other powers — Russian, French, British and Austrian — were gaining strength and influence in the area. In 1797 General Napoleon Bonaparte occupied Venice and all the Ionian Islands, and by the Treaty of Campo Formio that same year had all its Ionian possessions transferred to Austria.

> I stood in Venice on the Bridge of Sighs;
> A palace and a prison on each hand;
> I saw from out the wave her structures rise;
> As from the stroke of the enchanter's wand;
> A thousand years their cloudy wings expand
> Around me, and a dying glory smiles
> O'er the far times, when many a subject land
> Look'd to the winged Lion's marble piles,
> Where Venice sate in state, throned on her thousand isles!
> (Byron, *Childe Harold's Pilgrimage* IV)

The British The Napoleonic Wars were a confusing time for the Ionian islands. British victory over the French fleet at the Battle of the Nile in 1798 allowed their Russian and Turkish allies to capture the islands, and in 1800 to establish an 'independent' Septinsular Republic under Russian 'protection' — which took the form of a 10,000 man garrison. This was overturned in 1807 by the Treaty of Tilsit, which returned them to the bythen Emperor Napoleon, even though they were not strictly the Tsar's to concede. But in 1809 Kefallonia, Ithaka and Zakynthos were taken by the British, who held them and (eventually) the rest of the islands until the end of the war, after which the occupation was legitimised by the Congress of Vienna in 1815.

Meanwhile as Turkish power waned, so ideas of freedom fermented throughout the Balkans, and local Greek patriots began to combine forces with brigands *(klephts)* and outlaws to free their country. At the same time satellite Ottoman rulers became too

Part of the British cemetery on the outskirts of Zakynthos town. The inscription is to the memory of the wife and child of Lieut. Colonel Gubbins, 75th Regiment, 1820.

powerful to be controlled from Constantinople. A revolution proclaimed at Patras in 1821 was initially put down by Mehmet Ali, Pasha of Egypt, in return for the Sultan allowing him to occupy Crete as well as the Peloponnese. He nearly succeeded in crushing the revolution altogether, until Britain, France and Russia fortuitously combined to defeat him at the naval battle of Navarino, off Pylos in 1827. An earlier Protocol to give the Greeks an autonomous status within unspecified boundaries was imposed on Turkey after its further military defeats by Russia, and implemented in 1829. By 1833 the northern frontier had been fixed to run from Volos to Arta, and Otto, younger son of King Ludwig I of Bavaria, arrived in Athens — then with a population of 6,000 — to become first King of Greece as Otho I.

British rule continued its patronising and frequently autocratic ways in the Ionian — Napier (see Chapter 10) was informed by London 'You may plant an olive tree on Cephalonia and safely calculate on being able to repose in its shade while under the present Protectorate'. But olive trees tend to outlive political preconceptions! Economic mismanagement combined with Hellenistic fervour to fuel local discontent, whilst calculations of strategic requirement increasingly showed that possession of the islands was costing the country more than their worth. Mr Gladstone was appointed Lord High Commissioner Extraordinary in 1858 with a brief to sort things out, and reluctantly concluded their return to Greece was inevitable. The deposition of King Otho in 1862 and the need to find an anglophile replacement gave Palmerston the opportunity he needed. Prince William of Denmark, brother of Princess Alexandra — wife of the future King Edward VII — was put forward. In 1863 he was enthroned as George I of Greece, and the following year Britain formally returned the Ionian islands to Greece amid scenes of the wildest rejoicing.

1881 Thessaly and Epirus are returned from Turkey to Greece.
1912-13 A Balkan war gives Greece the opportunity to recapture Macedonia and the North Aegean islands.
1916 Greece enters the First World War on the side of the Allies: Turkey sides with Germany.
1921-22 Greece takes advantage of Turkey's defeat to invade, with the aim of 'liberating' all the Greek-speaking lands of Asia Minor. The plan misfires, as the Turks under Kemal Atatürk drive the Greeks 'back into the sea'. Hundreds of thousands of Greek civilians massacred in Turkey. The Greek king abdicates, and his

government falls. A military junta negotiates a vast exchange of populations. More than 1½ million refugees resettled in Greece. Smaller numbers of Turkish-speaking Greeks removed to Turkey.

1940 Italian, and then German, troops occupy Greece during the Second World War.

1945 Allied victory leads to the return of the Dodecanese from Italy.

1947 A civil war eventually resolves in Conservative governments and outlawing of the Communist Party.

1965 Election of a Liberal government under George Papandreou precipitates a constitutional struggle with the Monarchy, leading to..

1967 The Colonels' Military Coup. A Junta suppresses democracy for seven years, until ended by student riots and, more immediately, Turkish invasion of the northern part of Cyprus.

1974 Election of a Conservative government under Constantine Karamanlis.

1980 Karamanlis elected President.

1981 Socialist government of PASOK party under Andreas Papandreou.

1986 Greece joins the European Economic Community.

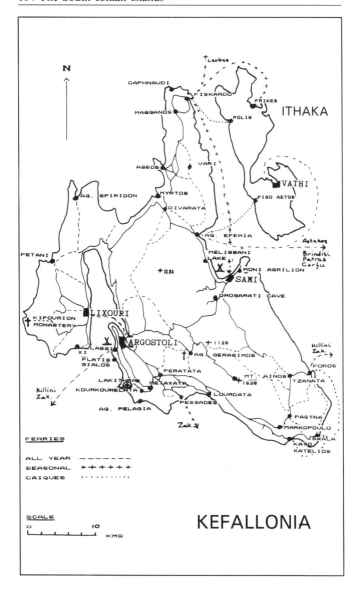

N

DAPHNAUDI

FISKARDO

FRIKES

ITHAKA

MAGGANOS

POLIS

ASSOS

VARI

VATHI

AG. SPIRIDON

MYRTOS

PISO AETOS

DIVARATA

AG. EFEMIA

Astakos →

PETANI

MELISSANI
LAKE

Brindisi
Patras
Corfu

+1131

MONI AGRILION

SAMI

DROGARATI CAVE

KIPOURION
MONASTERY

LIXOURI

ARGOSTOLI

+1125

Killini
Zak. →

LASSI

XI

AG. GERASIMOS

POROS

FLATIS
GIALOS

PERATATA

MT.
AINOS
1628

TZANATA

LAKITHRA

METAXATA

Killini
Zak.

KOURKOUMELATA

LOURDATA

PESSADES

PASTRA

AG. PELAGIA

Zak. →

MARKOPOULO

SKALA

KATO
KATELIOS

FERRIES

ALL YEAR   — — — — —
SEASONAL   + + + + +
CAIQUES   · · · · · · · · · ·

SCALE
0   10
          KMS

KEFALLONIA

TEN

Kefallonia

Population: 27,649   *Highest point: 1,628m*
Area: 781 sq km   *Hotel beds: 2572*

Kefallonia is a very large island, and everything about it is big. The statistics alone are impressive enough. It is indisputably the largest Ionian island: 30 per cent bigger than Corfu; almost twice the size of Zakynthos (although its population is smaller); more than twice as big as Levkas, and eight times bigger than Ithaka. But there is more to it than these two dimensions, since inland heights and ocean depths, mountains and valleys, are all built to this same massive scale.

Descending for a brief moment into trivia — something not easy in the context — the island may well hold some sort of a record for the number of different spellings of its name in common use. The first letter may be a K or a C; the F may be FF or PH; the L may be single or double; the O can be substituted by an I or E — between them these can give rise to over twenty permutations. None of them, fortunately, is likely to be mistaken for any other island.

Much of the island is mountainous, and its areas of level fertile ground — together with the larger towns to which they gave rise are few and far between. Away from these few plains the ground is not well structured to retain rainfall, and there are no rivers of significance. This is the main reason why traditionally an unusually large number of islanders left to make their own way on the mainland or overseas. Kefallonians have a reputation throughout Greece for their drive and aggression: whilst these qualities are unlikely to strike a visitor to the island, they may help to account for the success of islanders when away from it. Long is the list of national politicians, professors, teachers, business and commercial magnates, whose names are admired throughout the island for their achievements. Emigration has reduced the population by more than half since the beginning of the century; and although the decline has probably now halted, we cannot be sure until after the next 10-year census in 1991. But most of those who leave do so with every intention of coming back ... some day. And many do — even if in one of those motor hearses you'll sometimes encounter coming over on the ferry.

The island has been an important administrative centre since 800AD. Although Corfu was usually chief of the Ionian islands, if only because it lay closest to the occupying power, its position at the northern fringe necessitated a southern centre too, which fell to Kefallonia. Thus even today the nome of Kefallonia embraces Ithaka which actually has to share a telephone prefix with its giant neighbour. And until a decade ago it was responsible for all the islands between it and the mainland. The list still extends to a dozen, apart from Ithaka, though according to the census only two of them are inhabited, each by one person no doubt the lighthouse keeper! But the more populous Kalamos and Kastos are now very properly under the administration of Levkas.

Tourism is important, though not as the major industry it is in Zakynthos. Its largest concentration is found between Argostoli and the nearby airport, attracted there by some particularly fine beaches. There is a small pocket at Poros, but elsewhere tourist hotels are scattered thinly indeed. Moreover some two decades were to elapse after 1953 and its devastating earthquake, when reconstruction of the island was the overwhelming preoccupation of everybody: sensibly, not too much effort was made to attract tourism during those dark days.

In ancient times Kefallonia supported four cities Kranoi, Pale, Same and Pronoi whose present day successors are Argostoli, Lixouri, Sami and Poros respectively. These were situated widely apart, and since overland travel between them in those earlier days was difficult or even impossible, the only effective means of communication was by sea. Indeed one theory for reconciling some geographical implausibilities of the Odyssey postulates that Homer imagined each of them as chief city of its own island (see Chapter 11 for a more comprehensive discussion). This separation continues to some extent even today, and so it is convenient to consider the four modern towns and their surrounding hinterlands individually, together with a fifth area comprising the northern peninsula, where there seems not to have been an ancient city.

Arrival by air

The airport is situated 8kms from the centre of Argostoli, and opened its runway to international flights at the beginning of the 1980s. Since then traffic has increased considerably, mainly because of the growth in charter flights from the UK and other countries in north-west Europe. The present small and rather primitive terminal building is being replaced by a much larger concrete structure, which should be completed in time for the 1989 holiday season. Domestic flights are met by Olympic Airways buses, charter by their tour operators.

A summary of arrivals is:

● Domestic

From Athens: 1-2 flights each day by Boeing 737. Duration 50mins. From Zakynthos and Corfu: Some of the flights from Athens to Kefallonia continue on to Zakynthos; similarly some Athens-Zakynthos flights, also by Boeing 737, continue to Kefallonia. Additionally there are a couple of inter-island flights each week from Corfu to Kefallonia and Zakynthos, by tiny Dornier 228 aircraft. Together these give an approximately daily connection to and from Zakynthos, besides a twice-weekly service to Corfu.

● Charter flights

Up to 20 flights weekly from countries in north-west Europe are projected for the summer of 1989, about half of them from the UK. British regional airports include Gatwick, Birmingham, Cardiff, Luton and Manchester.

Arrival by sea

Kefallonia is unique among Greek islands, even Crete, for the number of its ports. Today there are no fewer than seven, six of them with scheduled services outside the island, five to the mainland (including Levkas).

The very advantageous tourist-oriented island-hopping summer service from Brindisi to Sami is discussed in chapter 3. It is operated by Seven Islands Travel with (currently) *C/F Ionis* and *C/F Ionian Glory*. Also mentioned in chapter 3 are the occasional calls there during a few peak season weeks by one of Hellenic Mediterranean Line's ferries. In the past Adriatic Ferries made similar calls with their *C/F Adriatic Star*.

Sami has always been the traditional arrival port from the mainland, its east coast situation and proximity to Ithaka making it the most convenient to the inter-island route between Patras and Corfu. There is a good sheltered harbour here, but without its ferry traffic the town would have been of minor importance only — for most passengers arrive here only to continue their journey to somewhere else. But Strinzis and Hellenic Coastal Lines continue to operate this Patras route with the *C/F Kefallinia* and *C/F Ionis* etc, on their way to Ithaka and (sometimes) Paxos and Corfu.

Argostoli has in recent times been alone among Greek island capital ports in having no external ferry services whatever, despite its excellent harbour. But this has now been rectified with the introduction of the *C/F Argostoli* on a route from Killini, operated by Seven Islands Travel.

Poros is the nearest port to the Peloponnese, but a tiny harbour seemed to preclude its use by any modern commercially-viable ferry. But since its enlargement in 1984 following a major dredging programme, Strinzis Lines' *C/F Ainos* — a former French ferry of optimum size and manoeuvrability for the task — now uses it for a second service to the island from Killini. In 1989 the same company's *C/F Delos* was operating the route instead. Poros is also the port used by the little *C/F Paxi* for its summer excursions from Zakynthos town.

Also in 1984, a new mainland service to Astakos was pioneered from **Ag. Efemia.** This small port is situated at the north end of Sami Bay, where an overnight berth for the *C/F Thiaki* is available. The ship calls at Ithaka on the way.

Further routes were then developed from the north of the island to Levkas (where motorists now drive across a man-made canal to the mainland, as discussed in chapters 3 and 12). Currently there are two, both operated by open deck car ferries. *C/F Aphrodite L,* based in Sami, crosses from **Fiskardo** to Vassiliki (Levkas). *C/F Meganisi* operates a triangular route from Nidri (Levkas) to **Fiskardo** and Frikes (Ithaka).

The most recent introduction is from **Pessades,** a tiny remote port some 15kms south west of Argostoli. Construction of a small concrete apron against which a ferry can thrust its bow for berthing now permits the *C/F Mana Barbara* to operate a summer service to the small port of Skinari in the north of Zakynthos. The ferry is based in **Lixouri,** where it can be boarded for the first run of the day, or disembarked from after the last. There is as yet no local ticket office, so motorists would be wise to make reservations with an Argostoli (or Lixouri) travel agent.

Summary of ferries
● From Italy
— Brindisi-Sami. 3 x weekly June & Sept, daily July & August. 15-18hrs. Fares: pax. from 5000drs, cars from 5500drs. *C/F Ionis, C/F Ionian Glory* +.
● From the Greek mainland
— Patras-Sami. Daily all year. 3½hrs. Fares: pax. 1025drs, cars from 4266drs. *C/F Ionis, C/F Kefallinia* +.
— Killini-Poros. 2-3 x daily all year. 1½hrs. Fares: pax. 536drs, cars 2922drs. *C/F Ainos.*
— Killini-Argostoli. 2 x daily all year. 2¾hrs. Fares: pax. 872drs, cars 3428 drs +. *C/F Argostoli.*
— Astakos-Ag. Efemia. Daily all year. 3½hrs. Fares: pax. 590drs, cars 3041drs. *C/F Thiaki.*
— Levkas(Nidri)-Fiskardo. 2 x daily April to Sept, 2 x 3 days a week in Oct. 1½hrs +. Fares: pax. 371drs, cars 2041drs. *C/F Meganisi, C/F Levkas.*
— Levkas(Vassiliki)-Fiskardo (continuing to Sami). 2 x daily June-Sept. 1hr. Fares: pax. 319drs, card 1320drs. *C/F Aphrodite L.*
● From the islands
— Corfu and Paxos-Sami. See *C/F Ionis* and *C/F Ionian Glory* above.
— Levkas-Fiskardo. See Nidri and Vassiliki above.
— Ithaka (Vathi)-Sami. See Patras-Sami above. 1½hrs. Fares: pax. 395drs, cars 2961drs.
— Ithaka(Frikes)-Fiskardo. See Levkas (Nidri)-Fiskardo above. ¾hr.
— Zakynthos town-Poros. 3 x weekly April-Sept. 2hrs. *C/F Paxi.*
— Zakynthos (Skinari)-Pessades. 2 x daily July & Aug, 2 x 3 days a week June & Sept. 1hr + *C/F Mana Barbara.*
— Zakynthos town-Argostoli. Chance of some summer sailings by *C/F Martha.*

In any emergency caiques can be chartered to run across from Ithaka, on the route Stavros (Polis)-Fiskardo, and possibly Piso Aetos-Ag. Efemia or Sami.

Getting about

The island has a satisfactory road system, although over long distances you may often wish for faster and more comfortable conditions. The best road is between Argostoli and Sami — actually a national responsibility, since it is the beginning of the traditional route to Athens. The other principal roads are from Argostoli to Poros along the south coast, and to Fiskardo in the north. A branch from the latter at Divarata provides the best route to Ag. Efemia, as well as an alternative way to Sami avoiding the mountains.

The road round the head of Argostoli Bay down to Lixouri is perfectly adequate; but since this route between the two towns is five times longer than the distance by sea, most people use the ferry instead.

Part of the road between Sami and Poros was till lately in a deplorable condition, though work had been in progress for some years to regrade it. Hard surfacing was still not complete in 1988, but its general condition had improved sufficiently for excursion buses from Poros to use it regularly, in a circuit of the southern part of the island.

Near Argostoli and Lixouri there are a large number of minor roads. Both the maps on sale locally are rather unreliable about these; but it's not difficult to find your way from signposts, and by asking if necessary.

Finding a petrol station should not be a problem, except perhaps in the north of the island — where, apart from Ag. Efemia, the only one is at Enosis, 11kms before Fiskardo. Even so, in Kefallonia it's wise not to let your petrol tank run low.

Buses

The island has an unusually enterprising KTEL bus company, situated on the waterfront at Argostoli. Not only does it maintain a bus information desk where English is spoken, but each year it prints a handsome colour leaflet setting out its routes, timings and fares, both in Greek and English. In summer it even runs excursion tours with an English-speaking guide, currently one to internal beauty spots and another across to Ithaka.

Four buses leave each day for Athens or Patras, which can be boarded in Argostoli (one of them starts in Lixouri). These buses cross on ferries from Argostoli or Poros to Killini, or from Sami to Patras. Should a single bus be insufficient, a duplicate or even triplicate is laid on. Internal buses to Ag. Efemia are also timed to connect with the ferry: although they do not cross, another bus is waiting on the other side.

Services within the island are summarised in the sections about Argostoli and Sami.

Hire of cars and bikes

Cars are easily hired in Argostoli, and Poros too, as also are the more powerful types of motorbike. Until quite recently it was difficult to hire mopeds because of their inability to cope with the gradients and distances. Nor for similar reasons have bicycles been available for hire — Kefallonia is simply not the place to bicycle for pleasure. But some mopeds have now appeared for strictly local use, as they have too at Lixouri, where local conditions are altogether more appropriate. But do make sure that whatever you hire is powerful enough for your intended purpose; it's not at all unusual to come across a car or bike broken-down beside some remote mountain road — where help can be a long time coming. Rental prices realistically reflect this wear and tear, as well as high recovery costs.

Taxis

Several hundred taxis are well-distributed among the towns and larger villages.

Argostoli and its environs

Argostoli is the island capital, a status thrust upon it in 1765 after the inland castle of St George — seat of the Venetian government and its supporting garrison — had been badly damaged by earthquake. Although described at the time as a miserable little village, Argostoli developed during the eighteenth and nineteenth centuries to become one of the most beautiful island capitals in Greece. On 12th August 1953 it was itself shattered by an even more devastating earthquake, which left not a single structure undamaged — apart from the stone causeway across its inner harbour, built by the British in 1813.

Since that dreadful day the town (and indeed much of the island) has been totally reconstructed, mainly by the efforts of Kefallonians themselves — islanders and expatriates — helped by funds from the Greek government and some foreign countries. A few buildings have been restored to a semblance of their former glory. But with the benefit of hindsight one can regret that greater efforts were not made at the beginning to recapture that previous ambience — especially by contrast with the admirable achievement in Zakynthos. Yet each year brings some further embellishment and improvement; and today Argostoli is no less attractive than other comparable towns on some Aegean islands.

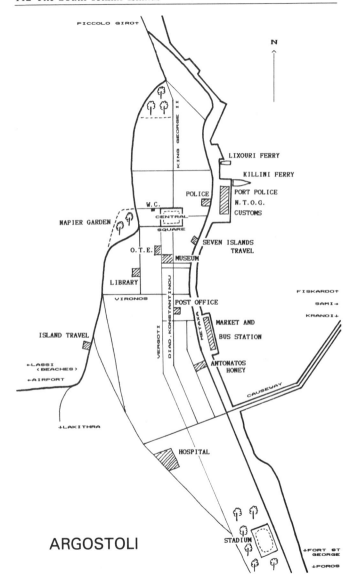

PICCOLO GIRO↑

N

KING GEORGE II

LIXOURI FERRY

KILLINI FERRY

PORT POLICE

POLICE

N.T.O.G.

W.C.

CUSTOMS

CENTRAL

SQUARE

NAPIER GARDEN

SEVEN ISLANDS
TRAVEL

O.T.E.

MUSEUM

LIBRARY

FISKARDO↑

VIRONOS

POST OFFICE

SAMI→

KRANOI↓

METAXA

MARKET AND

ISLAND TRAVEL

BUS STATION

←LASSI
(BEACHES)

VERGOTI

DIAD.KONSTANTINOU

ANTONATOS
HONEY

←AIRPORT

CAUSEWAY

↓LAKITHRA

HOSPITAL

ARGOSTOLI

STADIUM

↓FORT ST
GEORGE

↓POROS

The Bay of Argostoli is so huge that its outer waters have scarcely ever been made use of, apart from occasional visits by massed squadrons of warships assembled at anchor for fleet regattas — a practice which continued even into the 1950s. The town itself seems to turn its back on the open sea, preferring to look inland across a narrow lagoon-like expanse of water to its substantial mountains beyond.

Practically all facilities of tourist interest are situated within a strip of town between the waterfront, a parallel street called Diadhohou Konstantinou, and the **Plateia Valianou Metaxa.** This last is the town's central square, and the fashionable place for eating and drinking. Large numbers of tables and chairs are set out on an inner paved area, serviced by one or other of the cafés and restaurants surrounding it. Several of these seem rather trendily expensive, by Greek standards; but O Kefalos, on the corner with Diad. Konstantinou, serves a wide range of well-cooked traditional dishes at realistic prices.

Roads radiate in all directions from the central square. The widest and most impressive, **King George II Avenue,** leads out of town to the north (see Piccolo Giro below). On the other side of the square its extension, **Diadhohou Konstantinou,** begins as an imposing setting for important administrative buildings. This street is still remembered by many as Lithostratos, so called because of the massive stones (Roman, from Same) with which it used to be paved. Despite increasing narrowness as it penetrates further into the town, it remains the principal shopping street, as it was in colonial times. It also contains the post office and the nearby church of **St Nicholas,** with the delicate bell tower, which ministers to the town's significant Roman Catholic minority — reconstructed of course, but impressive for its richness and intensity. The inner part of this street is barred to traffic for much of the day. Above it, opposite the stone causeway, is the island hospital.

The waterfront is called **Metaxa,** after the distinguished general, a native of Kefallonia, who was Prime Minister of Greece at the outbreak of the Second World War. Prominent on its seaward side are the market and adjoining bus station (with WC and 'left luggage' facilities). Opposite are most of the larger food shops and hardware stores, several of them spanning across to the street behind. A good balance is achieved between the needs of local people and of tourists; but the latter are often surprised to find all the food shops closed on Monday, Wednesday and Saturday evenings — a regulation not often observed in tourist areas elsewhere. There are some good-value cheaper places to eat in this part of the town.

Between the bus station and the ferry berths you pass most of the travel agencies, Seven Islands Travel being near to the ferries. The long building near the inter-island ferry berth contains customs, port police and an information office of the NTOG (recently moved here from the Town Hall). The ferry to Lixouri is 100m beyond. From here it is but a short walk back to the central square (WC just beyond its north-west corner). Overlooking the square from the hillside behind is the **Napier Garden,** an attractive public park named after General Sir Charles Napier, who spent eight productive years as Resident of Kefallonia during the 1820s; we shall meet him again in connection with Lord Byron. The road to the beaches and airport turns to the left and continues on over the hill.

Commercial greetings to tourists leaving Argostoli airport.
  'I think that I shall never see
    A billboard lovely as a tree.
  Perhaps unless the billboards fall,
    I'll never see a tree at all.'
Ogden Nash (1902-1971) Song of the Open Road

Museums

Argostoli has two museums of very contrasting character:

● Archeological Museum. A fine building containing material of Mycenaean, Classical, Roman and Byzantine periods, collected from all parts of the island. Open 0830-1400 daily except Tuesday. 200drs.

● Library, with Historical and Popular Museum. The splendid museum is situated in the basement of the library building. Many of the exhibits illustrate island life during the nineteenth century; a poignant display of photographs showing the town before and after the earthquake must also be seen. Labelling, in Greek and English, is comprehensive and illuminating. Open daily except Sunday; between June and August 0830-1300 and 1800-2000; rest of the year 0900-1430. 100drs.

The Koryalenios Library above includes various Victorian works in foreign languages — part of its founder's bequest — and a collection of Napier papers.

Lixouri ferry

Several medium size open deck car ferries based on Lixouri operate a service across the Bay of Argostoli. This runs all the year throughout daylight hours, every 1-1½ hours. Timings are displayed on a board near the ferry berth. Fares: pax 109drs, cars 510drs + (including driver).

Buses

Internal services from Argostoli in summer 1988 are shown in the table.

To Same - 5 daily	To Skala - 3 daily
Kourkoumelata - 5 daily	St. Gerasimos - 5 daily
Poros - 4 daily	Assos - 1 daily
Ag. Efemia - 2 daily	Fiskardo - 2 daily
Makris and Platis Gialos beaches - every hr 0930-1800	

Outside the town

Lord Byron, from his first arrival in Kefallonia in August 1823, was in great demand socially. '... we have moreover been treated in the kindest manner by all the authorities military and civil — from Colonel Napier the resident (whose name and fame you are aware

of) the officers of the 8th. and in short by all our own countrymen.
— Their hospitality both here and in Ithaca was rather oppressive
— for dinners kill a weakly stomached Gentleman.' (Letters).

The diversions arranged for him would have included excursions
on horseback (or had there been ladies in his party, by carriage)
around the 'Piccolo Giro' and the 'Gran Giro'. Today these two
circuits still serve admirably for visiting the sights in the Argostoli
area.

The Piccolo Giro This comprises a tour of some 8kms around the
end of the Lassi peninsula on which the town of Argostoli is
situated. Leaving by the Avenue George II, after 2kms we reach the
Katavotheres Sea Mill. Byron would have passed by in ignorance,
since this subterranean channel into which the sea used to pour was
not discovered until 1835. Soon afterwards it was harnessed to

*Water-wheel at the Katavothres, which once harnessed the power
available from seawater pouring into a hole in the ground for
such purposes as grinding corn and manufacturing ice.*

power a corn mill, one of whose iron water-wheels still remains. The power of the water flow continued to be tapped for various purposes until 1953, when upheavals caused by the earthquake reduced it to a trickle. The wheel has now been landscaped into a backdrop for the adjoining restaurant. The water reappears on the other side of the island at Melissani (see Sami below)

The gates of **Camping Argostoli** (see Camping below) are now passed on the left, as the small ornamental lighthouse of **St Theodore** appears on the right. This was constructed by British sappers while Napier was Resident, and restored after the earthquake.

The road doubles back to the south, passing through pine trees and olives. until a succession of hotels and villas on the right indicates that we have arrived at the magnificent white sandy beaches which form the heart of Argostoli's tourist complex. The famous two are **Makris Giallos** and **Platis Giallos** — literally the 'long sands' and the 'broad sands'. Byron would have found both names appropriate, but it's hard today to associate broad with the nondescript-shaped beach below the White Rocks hotel. For that the earthquake, which caused the entire beach area to subside, must be held responsible. There are several smaller beaches apart from the famous two, but most are stony or else not easily accessible. A wide range of watersports — windsurfing, sailing, parasailing and waterskiing — is usually available.

It's an easy 1½km ride or drive back over the hill into the town, and in summer there's a half-hourly bus service; at other times this rather unattractive walk is an incentive to hire your own transport.

The Gran Giro Whereas the Piccolo Giro could and still can be accomplished easily enough on a Sunday afternoon after an indulgent lunch, the Gran Giro calls for sterner measures. At its simplest it consists of a direct run out to the Castle of St George, and return by another road nearer the coast.

Leaving town by Metaxa for the south west, the hill on the left across the lagoon is the site of **ancient Kranoi.** The more interesting route there involves crossing the lagoon by the stone causeway (signposted Sami), and bearing right immediately. The buildings on the left are part of the town waterworks — no doubt the spring was a major reason for building the city on that particular hill. Behind them a rough path leads up to the walls, which extend for some 5kms. To the right a convenient section in tolerably good condition has been cleared from its accretions of undergrowth; naturally there's a fine view of the town.

Continuing round the head of the lagoon and turning left on rejoining the main road, the **Castle of St George** (Ag. Georgios) soon becomes conspicuous on a hill ahead, unmistakable on account of the canopy of pine trees now grown up inside its walls. This was an ideal site for an occupying garrison, easily defensible, and with an excellent lookout to the Bay of Argostoli and along the south coast. During the second world war it saw duty yet again as headquarters for the Italian military command — the Germans were later stationed at Lixouri. It was as a young man during that period that the elderly custodian learnt his still excellent Italian. There are two possible roads up the hill, the nearer through the extensive ruins of the former capital below the walls, the other through the modern village of Troiannata. As you arrive at the gateway to the fort the caretaker, who lives just outside, will probably come out and offer to show you around. There's no entrance fee, but he should be tipped.

The castle probably took on its present shape during the Frankish period, later to be extensively remodelled by the Venetians. Although today something of an empty shell, what does remain is in good order — indeed it's generally considered the best of its kind in the Ionian islands. In addition to a panoramic tour of the splendid walls, some dungeons and storerooms can be visited, and you can peer down at the entrance to secret passages which before the earthquake used to run underground to Argostoli and Svoronata.

The main road below is rejoined at Travliata, where the giro now turns south to pass through an Arcadian landscape known as the Livatho. Here the lack of an accurate map becomes particularly irritating, since some villages and a number of connecting roads are just not shown. **The Moni Ag. Andreas,** whose approach is clearly signposted after a few hundred metres on the left, turns out to be a nunnery, but can be visited for its Byzantine-style frescoes. Shortly after that, another diversion in the same direction to **Pessades** is easy enough, since not only are there some signposts for the ferry, but more eye-catching ones proclaim the **Kefallonia Game Farm** on its outskirts. This was recently created by Mr Sklavounos, an American tycoon now back in his native village. Sportsmen are attracted here from all over Greece to shoot pheasants and other game-birds bred specially for the purpose, and pay 2,000drs per bird for the privilege. This activity is attracting vehement opposition from the ecology movement, and in any case these same birds can be bought more cheaply in the Argostoli meat market! But the village and its minuscule port 1km beyond are attractive whether or not you are interested in shooting or taking the ferry to Zakynthos.

But students of archeology get little help from maps or signposts. There are several Mycenaean rock-cut tomb sites around **Lakithra** which were excavated early this century, near Mazarakata, Metaxata and Kokolata among others, but these need local help to find. The ridge road to the right taking you through Lakithra provides the shortest route back to Argostoli.

Continuing south instead you will probably find yourself in the straggling village of **Metaxata.** Byron passed this way, whilst he and his party were still living on board ship in the harbour, and liked it well enough to rent a villa sufficiently close to the capital to get his letters without delay, but far enough to escape the strain of its social round. Here during the final months of 1823 he enjoyed the last peaceful moments of his short life. 'I ... am here in a very pretty village between the Mountains and the sea waiting what Napoleon called the "March of Events". ... standing at the window of my apartment ... the calm though cool serenity of a beautiful and transparent Moonlight - showing the Islands — the Mountains — the Sea — with a distant outline of the Morea traced between the double Azure of the waves and skies — have quieted me enough to be able to write ...' (Letters / Journal in Cephallonia)

Odhos Byronos is not difficult to find, but the villa itself was yet one more victim of 1953; a plaque fixed to a gate opposite, inscribed 'Lord Byron's ivy' has been reported, but both plaque and ivy seem since to have vanished.

The adjoining village of **Kourkoumelata** provides a remarkable contrast. This post-1953 construction, whose style and facilities would be worthy of an American garden suburb, was entirely financed by the Vergotis shipping family.

There is yet more contrast in the next village, **Kalligata,** whose fortunes are intertwined with the winemaking enterprise of the Calliga company. Under the direction of Messrs John and Gerasimos Calligas, the winery has expanded phenomenally in recent years to meet the demand for its products. The most prestigious of these, Robola, is made from native Robola grapes grown at the exceptional height of 600m, mostly near Valsamata and Frangata in the high Omala valley. What with this altitude and the narrow tiered terraces needed for cultivation there, the harvest — traditionally on 20 August — generally yields little more than 500kgs per 1000 sq m. Only the first pressing is used for Robola wine, which is fermented naturally in water-cooled vats with a selection of local enzymes for 4-5 weeks; bottling begins in February. The resulting product is dry, but not too much so, at 11.5° of alcohol. In former times such wine often did not travel well, despite its high esteem when drunk on the island; but modern techniques (though involving the minimum possible use of chemicals) have overcome the problem — as its successful marketing in scores of countries throughout the world must testify.

Another white grape named Tsaoussi produces the sweeter Blanc de Blanc. Reds, rubies and ross are based on Mavrodaphni and Muscadet grapes.

The baroque church in Kalligata is worth looking at, so is the one at nearby **Domata,** with its carved wooden icon screen. The giro now continues to the west through Sivronata, where a road leads to a pleasant beach at **Ag. Pelagia.** Now we are practically back in tourist land, for as the road veers right to the north west, a spur to the left leads directly to the airport.

The car ferry **Ionis** *backing stern to the quayside at Sami. This ship is engaged all the year round, shuttling between Patras and Ithaka via Kefallonia, with seasonal extensions to Paxos and Corfu. Her sister ship* **Argostoli** *plies between Killini and Argostoli during the season.*

Accommodation

Hotels Three very large hotels define the the tourist zone on the Lassi peninsula. Nearest to Argostoli is the Mediterranée, a top-class traditional hotel, wonderfully situated above a spacious private beach. At the far end overlooking Platis Giallos is the White Rocks with its extensive bungalow complex. Between these two are dotted a number of smaller hotels. On the far side of the airport is the Irina (not to be confused with the much smaller Irilena at Lassi), in splendid isolation beside the beach at Ag. Pelagia.

On the other side of the hill the hotels in Argostoli are rather smaller — the more expensive ones near the central square, the cheaper around the bus station.

Hotels in and near Argostoli

Class	Name	Rooms	Tel. (code 0671)
● In the town			
B	Xenia	24	22233
C	Aegli	9	22522
C	Aenos	40	28013
C	Aghios Gerassimos	15	28697
C	Argostoli	20	28358
C	Armonia	13	22566
C	Castello	12	23250
C	Cephalonia Star	38	23180
C	Galaxias	11	24096
C	Mouikis	36	23032
C	Phocas	18	28100
C	Regina	21	23557
C	Tourist	21	22510
and 5 lower category hotels.			
● At Lassi			
A	Mediterranée	227	28761
C	Irilena	22	23172
C	Lassi	32	23126
C	Lorenzo	45	28783
and one lower category hotel.			
● At Platis Gialos			
A	White Rocks (Bungalows)	163	23167
● At Agia Pelagia			
B	Irina	170	41287

Villas Interspersed between the beach hotels are numerous villas to rent. Most of the better ones turn out to be on the books of the Greek Islands Club (66 High Street, Walton-on-Thames, KT12 1BU) and its local agent, the Island travel agency, situated in the conspicuous yellow building half-way up the hill on the road out of Argostoli.

Camping Kefallonia is fortunate to have two long-established and well-organised campsites on opposite sides of the island. Both are members of the Sunshine Camping Group, an association of independent Greek campsites offering discounts to campers using several of its listed sites, as well as a discount on Fragline ferry tickets. Camping Argostoli is near the tip of the Lassi peninsula, 2kms north of the town. Open April to October.

The best water in the area comes from a spring at Prokopata, 3kms beyond the stone causeway.

Argostoli to Poros (43kms)

After passing below the Castle of St George, the main road begins to skirt the massive bulk of Mount Ainos, an eastward traverse through its lower foothills giving frequent views of the south coast below. An early opportunity to go down there comes soon after Peratata, where a road to the right through Karavados brings you to a small attractive beach at **Ag. Thomas.** The next beach, below **Lourdata,** though better known, suffers from constricted development, since there's little shade nor anywhere to park, except at one of its tavernas.

Some 5kms after returning to the main road, a bold signpost draws attention to the **Moni Theotokou Sision** (corruption of Assisi, St Francis of). The modern monastery stands securely fenced 1km down the track — its barking dogs will alert a monk who might show you around if he thinks some conversation with you worth his effort. Ruins of its predecessor are a short distance beyond, in process of being recolonised by the encircling woodland. A steep track leads on down to a superb and totally deserted beach, fine sand fringed with mature trees — a perfect situation for 'camping sauvage'. There's even a watertap outside the new monastery.

Back on the main road a broad coastal shelf fringed with miles of sandy beach soon comes into view below. Little visited until recently because of poor access, a newly improved road now glides quite smoothly down the hillside, approached from a right fork before Atsoupades. The landscape turns out more undulating than expected, with small hamlets folded into valleys among olives and woodland. But **Kato Katelios,** an isolated little fishing port with a couple of pleasant restaurants, can hardly be missed, and surely stands to benefit from the new road. Six kilometres further on **Skala** already has the potential of an attractive resort, helped by a generous tree-planting programme, now matured. The place to stay is Peter Zapadis's small family hotel Scala, whose clients return there year after year. Directly opposite are remains of a second-century AD Roman villa, with mosaics in surprisingly good condition (key at the hotel). Slight remains of a sixth century BC temple can be found 2kms beyond. A short cut up from the plain to Pastra is at present too rough to be recommended.

Rejoining the main road, the next village after Atsoupades is **Markopoulo.** It's worth stopping here at any time to admire the view from this mountain-side balcony. But early each August the village becomes a lure for the curious and the superstitious, because of an annual emergence of snakes. The phenomenon is not understood by zoologists; but since the snakes are entirely harmless, carry small black crosses on their heads, and never fail to arrive at the church in time for the Feast of the Assumption of the Blessed Virgin Mary on 15 August, it is traditionally believed that miraculous properties transfer to whoever catches them. There's another tradition that remote ancestors of Marco Polo came originally from this village.

The road now turns north up a valley, before descending through another beyond Ag. Georgios. Both were luxuriant with pines, olives and fruit trees, until devastated by the fire which swept through this corner of the island in the summer of 1988. The olives will recover, and fruit trees can be replanted; but the pines, alas, are lost for ever. At Tzanata a still-not-quite finished road continues north over the mountains to Sami. The main road descends towards a narrow cleft between two encircling mountains — a dramatic example of the spectacular scenery of the island, especially in winter when a foaming torrent rages below the roadside — to debouch into the outskirts of Poros on the other side.

Poros

The position of Poros as the island's number two tourist centre seems somewhat perverse, given that better endowed alternatives in this part of the island remain so little developed. No doubt it happened because a port was already there, as it had been two millennia before, when Pronoi was a thriving city up on the hill overlooking it to the south. But what assets there are have been put to good use, and it has become a pleasant little beach resort, well-suited for quiet family holidays. The beaches are pebbly, though patches of sand are claimed at the northern end. Watersports — windsurfing, waterskiing, pedaloes — are usually available. As it matures, the central square on the waterfront grows more attractive.

A low hill separates the town from its port, and the road between is suitable for a evening stroll, to watch the skill with which the gallant Captain Dimitrios insinuates his ferry *Ainos* into its constricted mooring. The harbour is used by fishing caiques, which sometimes run excursions round to Skala and elsewhere.

Accommodation

Hotels at or near Poros

Class	Name	Rooms	Tel. (code 0674)
● At Poros			
B	Belvedere (Apartments)	26	
B	Hercules (Pension)	5	72351
C	Atros Poros	10	72205
C	Kefalos	29	72139
and 3 lower category hotels.			
● At Skala			
C	Skala	8	23972
C	Tara Beach (Bungalows)	28	23997

Poros has villas and rooms for rent. Rooms can be found at several of the south coast villages.

This part of the island has no campsites, but is well suited to free camping. Some source of water should not be difficult to find.

Argostoli to Sami (24kms)

After crossing the stone causeway over the lagoon the road turns inland towards the mountains. After 7kms and the first pass a good road to the right leads into the Omala valley. This goes through the winegrowing villages of Frangata and Valsamata — reconstructed with the help of British money after the earthquake — before arriving at the **Monastery of Ag. Gerasimos,** named after the patron saint of the island who died there in 1579. The monastery (closed 1300-1500) is much visited by Kefallonians, as demonstrated by the five bus services each day from Argostoli. There are special processions on 16 Aug and 20 Oct each year — anniversaries of the saint's death and beatification — when his mummified body is paraded up and down, watched by devotees who come from all over Greece.

The main road continues its spectacular course through the mountains, reaching a height of 550m at the Pass of Agrapidiaes. From there on it is downhill all the way if you are going directly to Sami, but twice as far again if you decide to take a diversion up to the top of **Mount Ainos** (1628m). With your own transport that is not difficult, since a surfaced road, not too steep, goes most of the way up. A particular attraction is the forest of Kefallonian pine *(Abies Cephalonica),* a species resembling a cedar and unique to the island. This forest once covered practically the entire mountain, but fires and felling over the centuries have diminished it to about 1000 hectares (2200 acres), most of it around the flattened summit. The road stops at a TV transmitter, leaving a further 4kms walk through the forest, where you might notice the remains of a shrine to Zeus, thought to date from the eighth century BC. On a clear day the panorama can be stupendous.

Eight kilometres beyond the Pass of Agrapidiaes a signpost draws attention to the **Drogarati Cave,** 1km up a road on the left. This stalactite cave was opened in 1963. Thanks to its acoustics and some clever lighting you can imagine you are in a subterranean cathedral from Disneyland, where elfine organists play music from Fantasia to an accompaniment of dripping water. Open 0900-2000; 120drs (children 60drs).

Two kilometres on the right an unfinished road leads south into the mountains, on a direct route to Poros (26kms, see page 124).

Sami

This is a small town splendidly situated at a sheltered corner of Sami Bay, its sea views foreclosed by the mountainous bulk of nearby Ithaka. The town itself is neat and spacious, having been rebuilt (with British help) after 1953. Its pulse is regulated by the daily half dozen or so arrivals and departures of ferries, mostly to and from Ithaka. These berth with stern to the long projecting jetty or (more likely in the case of those operated by Seven Islands Travel) at the waterfront near the office of their agent Valetta Travel.

Buses wait near wherever the ferry is berthed. In addition to the main-line route from Argostoli, Sami has its own bus whose schedule — however informal — is also ferry-related. This runs to Ag. Efemia, continuing on to Divarata (Siniori) on the other side of the island; by this means it contrives a connection with one or other of the services between Argostoli and Fiskardo or Assos.

The town is the third largest on the island, which entitles it to one of the three island hospitals. There is an OTE (phone) office.

Time spent waiting for a boat can be pleasantly occupied with a stroll along the unsurfaced motor track at the east end of town, leading out towards the far headland. There are opportunities for swimming in rocky coves below, and fine views of Ithaka. At a point where you first see across the headland, you can either continue to a small village ahead, or go down to a splendid isolated sandy bay to your right the beaches in the main bay are stony; or by doubling a short way back up the hill, you arrive at **Moni Agrilion** — actually a nunnery. Beyond, between the two hills overlooking the town, is the site of ancient Same, one-time capital of the entire island, destroyed by the Romans in 188 BC. Little more than some sections of its wall now remain.

Accommodation

There are three small centrally situated hotels, and a number of rooms to let.

Hotels at or near Sami

Class	Name	Rooms	Tel. (code 0674)
● At Sami			
C	Ionion	16	22035
and 2 lower category hotels.			
● At Agia Efemia			
C	Pylaros	10	61210
C	Logara (Apartments)	23	61202

Camping Caravomilos Beach, situated less than 1km towards Ag. Efemia, has entrances from both the main road (formal) and the beach path (informal). The site is well-established, with friendly competent management. Plenty of shade is provided by mature pollarded poplars, and above-average facilities include a number of electric points. Its restaurant too is as good as any in town. Member of the Sunshine Group. Open April to October.

Excursion to Ag. Efemia

Two kilometres beyond the campsite, the road to Ag. Efemia passes through the village of Karavomilos, at whose northern extremity the **Melissani Lake** is boldly signposted to the left. This curious and remarkable spectacle is situated at the bottom of a vast double underground cavern, to reach which a passage has been hewn through the rock down to the water's edge. Here your personal Charon waits to row you across his domain, whose limpid clear waters are tinged ultramarine by light penetrating through a fallen section of the roof. Be reassured, he'll bring you back within twenty minutes! Open daily 0900-1800 (0800-1700 in summer), 130drs (65drs children).

This is the water that started its journey at the Sea Mill outside Argostoli. Now diluted to little more than brackish, most continues underground to feed the Karavomilos pool on the other side of the road, whilst the remainder bubbles up a few yards out to sea.

Ag. Efemia achieved some importance during the nineteenth century as the most convenient port for Ithaka. Thus Lord Byron, newly arrived in Argostoli and eager to indulge himself: 'To pass the time we made a little excursion over the mountains to Saint Eufemia — by worse roads than I ever met in the course of some years of travel in rough places of many countries. — At Saint Eufemia we embarked for Ithaca ... We returned to Saint Eufemia and passed over to the monastery on the opposite side of the bay and proceeded next day to Argostoli by a better road than the path to Saint Eufemia. — The land journey was made on Mules.' (Letters). His crossing would have been by caique to Piso Aetos; and it had better be said that the night of his return would have been spent not in the Moni Agrilion nunnery, but at Ag. Fanendes, a now ruined monastery behind Sami.

The taming of the mountain road to Sami, and the lack of a west coast port in Ithaka capable of berthing modern ferries, diminished for some time the status of Ag. Efemia — though it continued to benefit from trade in the products of the rich agricultural valley of Pilaros behind it. It was fortunate though to suffer less from earthquake damage than Sami. Thus it retains something of the atmosphere of a pre-war Devon fishing port, with added colour from the luxuriant Mediterranean plant-life, and a couple of small hotels which enliven its single main street. The presence of the *C/F Thiaki* has helped restore the port towards its former position.

Argostoli to Fiskardo (50kms)

Turning left from the stone causeway, the drive towards the north is uneventful until the head of the bay is reached, where a left turn leads round to Lixouri. The main road now climbs to traverse a steeply plunging mountainside, its engineering fortunately quite good enough to permit enjoyment of some spectacular views ahead and behind. Any desire to find a way down should be restrained until after the detour to cross the Pilaros valley at Divarata (Sinori), for at the next village, Anomeria, a precipitous track gives access to the dazzling white sands of **Myrtos,** probably not quite the finest, but certainly the most photogenic beach on the island.

Viewed from above, the outline of the Assos peninsula now begins to take on the shape of a giant ace of spades. A good new road descends steeply past cypress, olives, carob and other evergreens, enlivened in summer by yellow broom and purple valerian. The little village is sculpted into the base of the hillside, its picturesque houses (a few of them restored since the earthquake) overlooking a low spit of land — a sheltered port of call for visiting yachts. The steep-cliffed peninsula opposite is encircled by the remains of its Venetian castle and protective walls; you can pass through the right-angled entrance to explore some rambling remnants of a market garden, established earlier this century during the castle's temporary duty as a prison. Be careful though as you wander, lest with head high in romantic imagery your foot stumble into one of the crumbling water-cisterns.

The village has a small hotel, tavernas and a number of rooms to let. One of the buses that comes this way each day goes all the way down to the village; the other two pause above on the main road, leaving you with a half-hour-walk — even longer going back up.

At Enosis with its rare petrol station an unsurfaced road doubles back inland to reach **Vari** after 6kms. At Ano Erissos on the

Myrtos Beach. This twisting, precipitous descent is typical of many such tantalising beaches in the Ionian islands, although here a couple of motor-caravans have successfully made the descent (but did they get back up again?)

outskirts of this isolated village you can find the only surviving Byzantine building on the island, a small chapel with fine wall-paintings (for entrance ask at a café opposite the Vari church). A southern continuation, for masochists only, passes the still-functioning monastery of Theotokou Thematon, and after skirting the mountain above Ag. Efemia and the Pilaros valley, completes its tortuous circuit at Divarata.

Northwards the vegetation becomes lusher, with dense stands of cypress and other conifers, myrtle and scrub-oak. The large village of **Magganos** contains a better supermarket than any in Fiskardo. The road curves round the tip of the peninsula to pass two splendid rock-lined beaches, called **Daphnaudi** and **Embalisi** — both clearly signposted.

Fiskardo

The long arduous road ends here, at a village widely considered the most attractive on the island. A number of factors support this judgement: high among them rate the village's good fortune to escape the 1953 earthquake almost untouched and its fine waterside situation at the end of a long sea inlet. Its historical aura derives from the long-dead warrior whose name it bears, and the mysterious origin of the two ancient towers on the rocky foreshore opposite. For here in 1085 died Robert Guiscard, knight and Norman adventurer extraordinary, who, had he lived, might have gone on to take for himself the imperial crown of Byzantium, in addition to the kingdoms in Sicily and southern Italy already seized by his family, with the help of a handful of well-armed mercenaries. How on earth these alien northerners came to dominate for a brief period this remote corner of the Mediterranean is discussed in Chapter 9.

Since those heady days Fiskardo slept, only recently to be awakened by other invaders, come from distant parts in splendid yachts, more numerous even than the Normans. From their gold, gladly pocketed, it has benefited; but in the process much of its innocence has been lost. It is very much to the credit of certain individuals of outsize personality — such as Tassou of the Captain's Cabin, and Gerry at the original village shop — that the place continues to enjoy something of a happy family atmosphere. Despite boutiques and souvenir shops, and fishing caiques elbowed away from prime moorings, somehow Fiskardo has remained beautiful, still worthy of a visit, whatever the difficulty.

For Fiskardo caters primarily for its floating population, and makes little provision for land-lubbers to stay there long. Naturally there are plenty of waterside café and restaurants, and money can be changed at the post office (near the ferry berth) and at some shops and restaurants.

The two ferries calling at Fiskardo berth at the head of the creek, on the northern outskirt of the village. They go to Levkas (Vassiliki and Nidri), Ithaka (Frikes) and Sami. Caiques can be chartered in emergency for Ithaka (Stavros (Polis)). Excursion caiques from Levkas also call here from time to time.

The twice-daily bus service from Argostoli allows for the possibility of an afternoon visit.

Accommodation
This is a major difficulty; the only hotel is small and usually fully booked, and the number of rooms to let is quite inadequate to meet summer demand. The 'traditional settlement' scheme operated by the NGOT has now concluded, its buildings given back, fully restored, to their owners. Major changes are unlikely, since much of the ground belongs to absentee landlords.

Hotels at Fiskardo

Class	Name	Rooms	Tel. (code 0674)
B	Panormos (Pension)	6	51340

Camping There are no campsites, but free camping is certainly possible at various beaches outside the village. These are often surrounded by smooth flat-topped rocks, upon which the supple can sunbathe by day and sleep by night. Water is a major limitation, the traditional shortage exacerbated by fissuring of the water-table in 1953.

Lixouri and the Paliki peninsula

Shaped like the claw of a lobster, this appendage to Kefallonia is little visited by tourists, since no obvious reason exists for doing so. But those with time and (preferably) independent transport have the opportunity to discover an area quite different from the rest of the island. From Argostoli it is convenient to cross on the ferry, since most possible objectives lie in the south. Tickets are bought on the boat.

The ferry berths at the centre of **Lixouri,** practically opposite the small main square. From here depart the buses, but not (as yet) to places of much interest to tourists. Mopeds can be rented, and taxis hired. Lixouri itself, though second only to Argostoli, is a work-a-day little town, whose hotels cater more for agricultural salesmen than tourists. But it has a **museum** containing local finds mainly from Pali, with an occasional label in English. Open 0800-1430 (Sun. 0900-1400) closed Tues. 100drs. **Pali,** which gave its name to the entire peninsula, was once a city of some importance. Its site is up the coast 2kms to the north, but little now remains except its recycled stone used in the modern town.

The road network of the Paliki peninsula has been, apart from a few sections, unsurfaced and in generally poor condition. An improvement programme is in progress, but it's hard to select the best routes without knowing the extent of current progress. Four roads fan out away from the town.

The first goes south down the coast towards a number of beaches, mostly untouched by tourism. Several sandy coves face across to Argostoli, but the biggest and best beach called **Xi,** famous for its reddish sand, is round the other side of the Ag. Georgios headland. Beaches beyond are probably best approached from the second road.

This starts off four blocks inland and parallel with the first, before turning south west, eventually to complete a circuit back to the capital. At Mantzavinata a fork leads south to **Kounopetra,** named after another of those geological phenomena for which Kefallonia is celebrated — a large low rock in the sea which used to oscillate from side to side. Since 1953 it has moved no more. But the nearby Ionian Sea hotel enjoys its prestige, and the benefit of another splendid beach in the shelter of the southern headland.

The main road continues through chalky eroded burnt-up landscape, which turns out to be surprisingly well-suited to the cultivation of currant vines. Tarmac ceased at Chavriata, where it veers north to Chavdata (on the bus route, direct from Lixouri). Halfway between the two a left fork runs westward over some bare hills. Taking the second turn on the left after a quarry, an isolated wooded valley appears almost as a mirage; but it is real enough, thanks to generations of monks who cherished its fertility from the now deserted Tafios monastery at its top. The remaining monks have moved down to the newer **Kipourion monastery,** spectacularly high on a fertile ledge overlooking the sea. The building is attractive, though purists regret some over-zealous restoration. A block of cells is reserved for over-night guests (donation appropriate). The monks seem quite tolerant about dress regulations.

The third road leads up into the hills to the north west; the town buses have hitherto mainly confined their services to villages on or near it, which get visited three or four times daily. **Monopolata** is one of the more attractive of these. Other villages on the bus route are Kaminarata, Damoulianata, Skineas and **Kontogenada,** which enjoys fine views back over the Bay of Argostoli, and where the road terminates. But an extension back to the head of the bay, which is already quite serviceable, has opened up another fine beach called **Petani.**

The fourth main road, now resurfaced throughout, runs north beside the shore of the bay. A poor extension continues up to the top of the peninsula, ending at the isolated but pleasant little village of **Ag. Spiridon;** its potentially attractive beach below tends to collect debris blown in on the prevailing north-west winds.

Hotels at or near Lixouri

Class	Name	Rooms	Tel. (code 0671)
● At Lixouri			
B	Il Giardino (Apartments)	7	92505
C	Poseidon	35	92518
C	Summery	56	91771
● At Kounopetra			
B	Ionian Sea	24	92280

Island products

The chief industry of Kefallonia remains agriculture, and very little suitable land remains uncultivated. The best of it, often terraced, is used for wheat, or an occasional crop of tobacco. Olive trees and the currant vine are important; but the story of their establishment and development under the Venetians is reserved for Zakynthos (Chapter 13), where they were even more important. Grapes for wine-making have already been mentioned on page 00. Almonds and other nuts are grown, which are made into a confection called *mandoles.*

Whilst the greater part of the land cannot be cultivated at all, the chances are that it contains a fair population of aromatic flowering plants attractive to bees, despite its parched and barren look. For

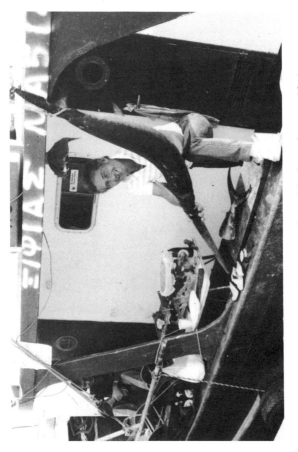

Caique captain selling his catch direct to the public from the quayside in Argostoli. He does a brisk trade in swordfish, one of which he obligingly displays for the author.

over a century now four villages on mountain slopes overlooking Argostoli Bay have specialised in bee-keeping, and all that time members of the Antonatos family have been going up there to collect and sell their honey. The best and most delicious grade is produced by bees feeding exclusively on thyme. This is packaged into bottles and tins under the 'Golden Honey' brand name, for sale from the Antonatos shop opposite the bus station, elsewhere on the island, and in Patras and Athens. Honey produced further north is collected at St Efemia, where it can be bought direct out of bulk containers.

Citrus trees grow well in parts of the south coast and elsewhere, and these provide the basis for lemon and orange drinks made in Lixouri and Argostoli, sold as *lemonada* and *portokalada*.

Three dishes special to the island are occasionally seen on restaurant menus. *Kreetopitta* is a pie made from goat-meat cooked with rice and tomato, topped with pastry. *Bacaliarpitta* is a fish pie made from dried salted codfish, usually expensive because it takes a long time to prepare; it is normally accompanied by *skordalia,* a potato dish heavily flavoured with garlic.

Island festivities

Each village has its own local feast day, many of them during the summer. But the following are of more than local interest:

15 Aug	●	The Assumption of the Virgin. Celebrated generally, but especially at Markopoulo.
16 Aug	●	Death of Ag. Gerasimos. Processions at his monastery in the Omala.
20 Oct	●	Beatification of Ag. Gerasimos. Processions at his monastery in the Omala.

Lord Byron and Kefallonia

The history of Kefallonia differs only marginally from that of Zakynthos and Ithaka, which are discussed together in Chapter 9. But this is the moment to draw together the threads of Lord Byron's visit to the island, which has cropped up already in several parts of this chapter.

At a period in the early nineteenth century when the intellectual classes of Britain, France and Germany were intensely interested in their Greek heritage and the efforts of mainland Greeks to free themselves from Turkish domination, the part played by one individual must do duty for that of a whole society. To this role Byron is uniquely suited; through his thoughts and words, more intimately confided through his poetry than by any other writing in the English language; and by his deeds — his heroic work in raising large sums of money, much of it from his own pocket, and his ultimate sacrifice in the shadow of the battlefield. His brief intervention ensured that Europe could never again forget or abandon the Greeks.

From his first appearance there Byron began to scandalise London society with the promiscuity of his relationships 'mad, bad and dangerous to know', as he confided to his Journal. His assets were little more than a newly-inherited title and his irresistible good looks when he took himself off to tour southern Europe. He arrived in Patras in 1809 — wars of the French revolution notwithstanding — and quickly moved on to Athens and elsewhere. He poured these experiences into his works *Childe Harold* and *The Maid of Athens* — and woke up one morning to find himself famous and, for the first time in his life, financially secure. Giving instructions for the sale of his family seat, he took himself off to live in Italy, where he continued to lead the life of dissipation expected of him, an experience which was to fatally weaken him, as he eventually realised.

> But now at thirty years my hair is grey —
>   (I wonder what it will be like at forty?)
> I thought of a peruke the other day —
>   My heart is not much greener; and, in short, I
> Have squandered my whole summer while 'twas May ...
> (Don Juan CCXII)

The futility of his life now began to sickened him, and his dreams turned to some great deed by which posterity might remember him. During a visit to England Lord Byron became involved with the Philhellene movement, and was elected a member of the London Greek committee in April 1923.

> The sword, the banner, and the field,
>   Glory and Greece, around me see!
> The Spartan, borne upon his shield,
>   Was not more free.
>
> Awake! (not Greece, — she is awake!)
>   Awake my spirit! Think through whom
> Thy life-blood tracks its parent lake,
>   And then strikes home!

He bought a small ship in Genoa and set out with assorted companions and animals for the Ionian islands. Their intended destination had been Zakynthos, where he had a banker's introduction. But at Legorn he was joined by the Scot James Browne, who had served in the Ionian islands before being dismissed for his Hellenic sympathies. Browne recommended a change of course for Kefallonia, then governed by Colonel Charles Napier, the only English Resident openly to favour the Greek cause — a Colonel Napier who later wrote of Kefallonia in his diary: 'every hour not employed to do her good appears wasted'. And so on 2 August 1823 the tub *Hercules* dropped anchor off Argostoli.

During that autumn and early winter, whilst awaiting the 'march of events' in Kefallonia, Byron reached a final decision. On 4 Jan 1824 he sailed to join Prince Mavrocordatos at Missolonghi.

> If thou regret'st thy youth, why live?
>   The land of honourable death
> Is here: — up to the Field, and give
>   Away thy breath!
>
> Seek out — less often sought than found —
>   A soldier's grave, for thee the best;
> Then look around, and choose thy ground,
>   And take thy rest.

('On this day I complete my thirty-sixth year' Missolonghi 22 Jan 1824)

The final act of Byron's real life drama is described in Chapter 14, Missolonghi.

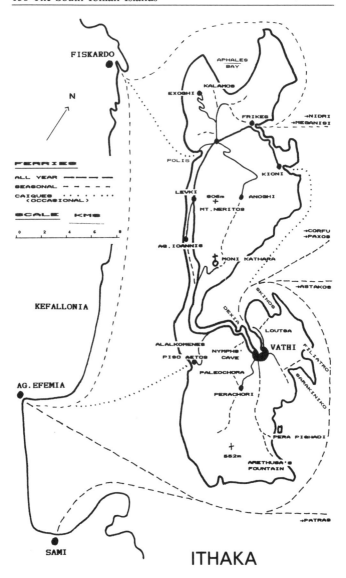

FISKARDO

N

APHALES
BAY

KALAMOS

EXOGHI

FRIKES →NIDRI
→MEGANISI

POLIS

KIONI

FERRIES

ALL YEAR ———
SEASONAL – – –
CAIQUES · · · · · · ·
(OCCASIONAL)

LEVKI 806m ANOGHI
+
MT. NERITOS

SCALE   KMS

0   2   4   6   8

AG. IOANNIS

→CORFU
→PAXOS

MONI KATHARA

→ASTAKOS

KEFALLONIA

SKINOS
DEXIA
LOUTSA

ALALKOMENES
NYMPHS VATHI
PISO AETOS CAVE

FILIATRO

PALEOCHORA

SARAKINIKO

AG. EFEMIA

PERACHORI

PERA PIGHADI

+
552m
ARETHUSA'S
FOUNTAIN

→PATRAS

SAMI

ITHAKA

ELEVEN

Ithaka

Population: 3,646 *Highest Point: 806m*
Area: 96 sq km *Hotel beds: 136*

The wonder of Ithaka is that more than one island lies waiting for
you to discover. You will see at once that Ithaka has two parts,
north and south, each with a separate identity, connected one to the
other by a barren ridge of rock ... but that was not my meaning.
Rather you will discover that its mountains and valleys, springs,
caves and beaches which you can enjoy today, are also interwoven
with those of another island — an island that exists only in the
imagination, whose substance is just a legend; yet a legend which,
when written, became one of the profoundest influences of our
western culture. For Ithaka is haunted by the great epic of
Odysseus. Facets from it continue to sparkle within world literature;
Ithaka stands synonymous with home and homesickness, destiny
and ultimate return. Time — much time — has passed since
Homer's day, yet the stories he told remain captive here, their
echoes always present, ready to be enjoyed by all who have ears to
hear them.

   The island is situated close to the northern peninsula of
Kefallonia, across a narrow channel whose width varies between 1
and 3 nautical miles. Its topography is varied, but is always on so
human a scale that people are not diminished. It has been inhabited
since the Neolithic period, although the number of its inhabitants
has fluctuated greatly, increasing when times were settled, and
falling almost to nothing when pirates or invaders were on the
rampage. Thus the Venetian inheritance at the beginning of the
sixteenth century was limited to a few dozen subjects, who had
multiplied to 10,000 by the time they left at the end of the
eighteenth. Under British rule the maximum of nearly 15,000 was
reached, from which it has fallen ever since — during this century

by an average of 100 every year. Though probably now stable, the present population level is low and includes a high proportion of the elderly. Cultivation of the land is often neglected in outlying parts — an opportunity perhaps for foreigners wishing to establish themselves on their own plot beside some distant part of the Mediterranean?

Most of the buildings were destroyed by the earthquake of 1953. During the painful recovery period tourism became important, although tourist numbers are small compared with the other islands. The main centre is **Kioni** in the north east, with a modest level of visitors in the capital, **Vathi.**

Administratively Ithaka is an eparchy, within the nome of Kefallonia. Politically it usually votes communist, as befits the only Ionian island where no aristocracy ever took root in colonial times. Its telephone prefix, 0674, is shared with the east part of Kefallonia.

During historical times the island has been known from time to time by various other names, such as Nerikii, Val di Compare and Thiaki. Today the island name is sometimes spelt Ithaca, or Ithaki.

Arrival by air

Ithaka has no airport of its own, but can be reached without too much difficulty from Kefallonia and Preveza (Aktion) airports. All the details you need are covered in Chapters 3, 4, 10 and 12.

Arrival by sea

Ithaka stands in the shadow of its giant neighbour, in matters of sea transport as in much else. But for that, its capital port, situated at the head of a fine sheltered deep-water harbour, would be ideally placed for connecting with the mainland. In reality ferries from Patras head directly for Sami in Kefallonia to discharge the major part of their cargo, before continuing to Vathi almost as an afterthought; so by the time the ferry has rounded the south of Ithaka and spiralled in through its long narrow entrance, the direct distance between the two ports has almost doubled.

Another problem at Vathi is that there is no proper jetty: ferries simply use the main road running out of town to load and unload, so the size of ship that can be used is limited by the depth of water. To construct a proper jetty would be no problem, except for justifying its cost.

These disadvantages notwithstanding, Vathi is the port of call for all the larger ferries calling at Ithaka. In summer it can be reached directly even from Italy, by means of the very advantageous tourist-oriented island-hopping service from Brindisi to Patras via most of the other Ionian islands (see page 00). Delas Tours (beside the ferry berth) is the agent for Seven Islands Travel, which operates the *C/F Ionis* and *C/F Ionian Glory*. Currently the latter does not call at Ithaka because of depth problems, but in future both chartered ships should do so. Other ferries run on domestic sectors of the route in summer. The rest of the year Strinzis and Hellenic Coastal Lines continue operations via Kefallonia with the *C/F Kefallinia* and *C/F Ionis,* some services going on to Corfu and Paxos, though in winter such incursions are rare. Vathi is also a port of call on the regular service from Kefallonia to Astakos on the mainland, run by the *C/F Thiaki.* (See Chapter 10)

Summary of ferries
● **From Italy.**
— Brindisi-Vathi. 3 x weekly June & Sept, daily July & August. 16hrs. Fares: pax. from 5000drs, cars from 5500drs. *C/F Ionis, C/F Ionian Glory.*
● **From the Greek mainland.**
— Patras-Vathi via Kefallonia. Daily + all year. 5½hrs. Fares: pax. 1025drs, cars 4416drs. *C/F Ionis, C/F Kefallinia* +.
● Astakos-Vathi. Daily all year. 1¾hrs. Fares: pax. 436drs, cars 2365drs. *C/F Thiaki.*
● **From the islands.**
— Corfu and Paxos-Vathi. See *C/F Ionis* and *C/F Ionian Glory* above.
— Kefallonia (Sami)-Vathi. See Patras-Vathi above. 1½hrs. Fares: pax. 395drs, cars 2961drs.
— Kefallonia (Ag. Efemia)-Vathi. See Askakos-Vathi above. 1½hrs.

Another route has developed from the north of the island to Levkas, where motorists can now cross the man-made canal to the mainland without risk of any significant delay. **Frikes** is a small village between Stavros and Kioni, conveniently situated at the head of a sheltered inlet. The open decked *C/F Meganisi* calls here on its triangular route from Nidri (Levkas) to Frikes and Fiskardo (Kefallonia) (see Chapters 3 and 12).

● **From Levkas.**
— Nidri-Frikes. 2 x daily April to Sept, 2 x 3 days a week in Oct. 1hrs +. Fares: pax. 371drs, cars 2041drs. *C/F Meganisi, C/F Levkas.*
● **From Kefallonia.**
— As from Levkas above, but once daily.

Until outgrown by modern ferries, two small east coast ports had been used since time immemorial for the crossing to Kefallonia. **Piso Aetos** to Ag. Efemia was the main link, whilst **Polis** was connected to Fiskardo. The few fishing caiques still based there are sometimes chartered to run across to Kefallonia in an emergency, usually from Polis.

Getting about

The roads of Ithaka are surprisingly good. The main route linking Vathi in the south with Kioni in the north is well-engineered and in good condition. Elsewhere there is a better proportion of tarmac and fewer pot-holes than on the other islands.

An island bus runs two or three times daily between Vathi and Kioni, but cannot entirely be relied on. And since a summer alternative that might suggest itself — the caique service between Kioni and Vathi — is even more spasmodic, it is fortunate that the number of taxis has been increasing, and now stands at 30. These can be treated almost as if they were small buses; one or more of them should be waiting when ferries arrive. Cars, scooters, mopeds and bicycles can be hired in Vathi, scooters and mopeds in Kioni and Frikes. The only petrol station is at Vathi — although obviously the hire firms elsewhere keep their own supply.

Centres of population

Vathi is a charmingly situated small town, with all the facilities to be expected of a minor island capital. Its focus is the caique and yacht harbour at the southern corner of the bay (where there's a public WC), together with the adjoining Main Square. Close to hand are the post and telephone offices, the Town Hall with its small information office, and a branch of the National Bank of Greece. From here the town spreads out in the shape of the horseshoe from which it takes its name. To the east 300m stands the Orthodox cathedral (Metropolis) built in 1800, with a good carved wood screen. Nearby is the Archeological Museum, closed for several years for major reconstruction and reorganisation, but now reopened. Exhibits are mainly from finds at Aetos in the south of the island, which have been newly catalogued with the help of Washington University (open 0900-1245, closed Saturday). A stele to Lord Byron in a courtyard outside carries the quotation 'If this island belonged to me I would bury all my books here and never go away.' There is a small hospital at the back of the town. The church of Taxiarchis has an icon of Christ reputedly by El Greco.

Before the Venetian occupation the island capital had been Paleochora, high on the hillside above Vathi, where you can scramble to discover its many ruined buildings which include several churches one whose Byzantine frescoes remain in amazing condition, considering they are totally exposed to the elements. But its population has long since moved down the hill, many to the agricultural and winemaking village of **Perachori,** which hosts a wine festival at the end of August. The Perachori-Vathi complex, where two thirds of the island population lives, is virtually the only inhabited area in the south part of the island.

A quiet road runs round the north of the bay, passing the fuel and supply station for yachts, various restaurants, cafés and bars, until it arrives at the Loutsa, at one time an important shipbuilding and repair centre. This is overlooked by the remains of a French fort hurredly built in 1807 — there was another on the opposite shore.

The main road out of town runs along the south of the bay, passing the ferry berths (400m beyond the Main Square) and the small island of Lazareto with its church of Sotiros (the Saviour) — a quarantine station during the English period and later a prison. Scartsoumponisi, another tiny island just outside the harbour entrance, also has its small church, Ag. Andreas. Beyond, on the lower slopes of Mount Neritos, with spectacular views back across the harbour to Vathi, stands the **Monastery of Kathara.** Although rebuilt after the earthquake, it has not been occupied by monks in recent years. Nevertheless arrangements are made to open it in summer to let visitors see some wall paintings, a reredos, and an icon attributed to St Luke. And people come from all over the island to its festival on 8 September, traditionally organised by the village of Anoghi.

Island festivities
Each village has its own local feast day, many of them during the summer. But the following are of more than local interest:

20 July	● Festival of Ag. Elias at Kioni.
5-6 Aug	● Festival of Sotiros at Stavros, the largest festival on the island.
end August	● Wine festival at Perachori.
8 September	● Festival of the Virgin Kathariotissa, at the monastery of Kathara.

The hub of the north part of the island is the nineteenth-century village of **Stavros,** which looks down to the bay of Polis and across to the mountains of Kefallonia. Situated 17kms from Vathi, it developed at the crossroads for the many small communities in its area, and so is more extensive than its permanent population of 300 would imply. The main square with its church of Sotiros hosts the biggest festival on the island at the beginning of August. A museum on its northern outskirts contains finds from the Pelikata ridge and Polis cave. This too has recently been reorganised; it should contain the fragments of the 12 bronze tripods (see below) as well as the votive offering to Odysseus, but the museum at Vathi also covets them. The key is kept at the village school — the English-speaking wife of its teacher acts as unofficial curator.

Two villages of earlier importance overlook Stavros. **Exogi** (meaning 'out of the earth'), 3kms to the north, is surrounded by potentially fertile terraces — but its former population of 1300 is now reduced to fewer than 100. There are superb views in all directions from the uninhabited monastery above it. **Anoghi** ('above the earth') is 5kms to the south east, and at 550m even higher. Its church of the Panaghia contains impressive paintings, some of them only lately revealed, after the earthquake had dislodged the plaster with which they were covered. The village was noted for the extent to which it had maintained its Venetian-influenced customs and dialect — somewhat isolated as it was by the diabolical condition of its access-road. But whilst the road has since improved, most of its inhabitants have in any case moved down to Kioni, to which it is connected by a scenic mule-track.

They can hardly be blamed for their desertion, for **Kioni** is a particularly attractive village. From its abandoned windmills at the top of the ridge, a mosaic drift of small traditional houses zig-zags

(**Above**) *Vathi harbour seen from the hillside to the south of the town. A sixteenth century bell-tower, one of many ruins forming the ancient capital of Paleochora, is clearly silhouetted against the calm waters of the harbour.* (**Below**) *View across the bay from Vathi harbour to the islet of Lazaretto.*

down to the fishing port below. Despite the highest concentration of tourism in the island, development has been quite tasteful and restrained, whilst traffic problems have been eased by a relief road skirting the village. Every summer finds it filled with foreigners, many from yachts moored in the bay; but others can still enjoy a simple seaside holiday there in one of the many villas available for rent. The bus and caique services to Vathi are convenient, when running.

Indeed the restraint at Kioni has presented something of an opportunity for **Frikes,** which is a pleasant 45-minute walk in the direction of Stavros. This tiny fishing and ferry port now boasts as many as three restaurants, of sufficient quality to draw evening visitors over from Kioni, as well as 'resident' yachtsmen from the flotilla of Greek Island Sailing Club. One of the island's few hotels is situated quite inconspicuously at the back of the village, but the former Club Méditerranée complex no longer exists.

Excursions and beaches

The island lends itself to exploration on foot, by bicycle and moped. In addition to several suitable objectives already mentioned, a beach picnic might be combined with a visit to one or more of the places associated with Homeric legend (see below). Some of the possibilities are described below, in clockwise sequence from the capital.

The south
— The nearest beaches to Vathi are along the north side of the bay, where mature shady trees and a variety of little places to eat and drink may compensate for stony shallows. The little-frequented **Skinos Bay** can be reached by an unmade track which passes over the ridge on your right as you approach Loutsa.
— Leaving Vathi by the road leading west past the cathedral, **Sarakiniko Bay** can first be seen on the left from the top of the ridge, whence it can be approached by unmade track. The beach is pebbles and sand, but your enjoyment may be disturbed by the activities of a hippie commune of young Germans who have been living out their version of 'the good life' there for some years. The next bay to the north, **Filiatro,** has a better beach which is outside the normal sphere of commune activity.

— The longer excursion to **Arethusa's Fountain** is begun along the road leading south past the hospital. The first 6kms of unmade track are straightforward, until a narrow path beyond the parking area slopes down towards the sea and an attractive small beach opposite the islet of **Pera Pighadi.** Another path takes you more parallel to the coastline towards the fountain where Eumaeus, faithful retainer of Odysseus, watered his pigs. In summer at least the fountain issues almost imperceptibly from a rocky ledge. The line of cliffs above is known as **Korax** or Ravens' Rock. Behind it you could find the cave once used by Eumaeus.

— Leaving Vathi by the main road along the south of the bay, after 3kms you come to the **Bay of Dexia,** shaped like a small horseshoe — its present-day status as a bathing beach is ensured by annual applications of imported sand. The signpost reads **Bay of Phorkys,**

The tiny fishing port of Frikes from the Meganisi ferry berth.

since this is the place where the sleeping Odysseus was put ashore by the Phaeacians. His first action after waking was to hide his presents and other objects in a cave. Such a cave is situated a good kilometre up on the hillside above, signposted 1km before Dexia as the **Cave of the Nymphs** (also known as Marmarospielia). This is open during the summer, and electric lighting now permits you to view its dominant stalagmite in safety. A cave beside Dexia itself would have been more convenient to Odysseus; one did exist there until the eighteenth century, when quarrying destroyed it.

—   One and a half kilometres beyond the bay of Dexia a well-surfaced road signposted **Piso Aetos** takes you over to the other side of the island. Some low remains of the walls of ancient Alalkomenes can be seen 300m to the right as you pass over the saddle. Schliemann came here to look, unsuccessfully for once, for the olive tree which Odysseus had used as a bedpost. Standing on this spot below Aetos and gazing out to sea you can understand the imagery of the eagle after which the mountain was named. The little port below is attractive; there is an unfrequented pebble beach beyond, where a few olive trees give some shade.

The north

— The main road to Stavros now avoids any need to descend to sea level by clinging to the steep slopes of Mt Neritos, an idea implemented during the British period. But the old road, which diverges a few yards before the turning to the Kathara monastery, can still be used to get down to **Ag. Ioannis,** despite its rough condition. Only five families live there, so you can be confident of getting one of several attractive shingle beaches all to yourself. The road up on the other side is both surfaced and rather less steep. It rejoins the main road at **Levki,** where you could wander down through this pretty village to several more beaches below.

— The **Bay of Polis,** below Stavros, has a sheltered shingle beach that is pleasant enough, but one would be more likely to come here for the Homeric vibrations. From its very name scholars believe a town of considerable importance must long ago have been close by. It is the north's candidate for the **Bay of Phorkys,** whilst from the cave of Louizou on its north-west side were found the fragments of the 12 (or 13) brass tripod vases (see below, though the cave itself is no longer worth trying to get at). But if you were to swim far out to the north-west headland on a calm day, you just might be able to see traces of the Byzantine city of Ierousalem, which subsided into the sea, probably after the earthquake of 967AD.

— The road between Stavros and Exogi leads past the so-called **School of Homer** (signposted). Its foundations appear to have been part of a sixth century BC tower, upon which was later built a chapel to Ag. Athanasios. The site juts out into the valley, looking down over the Spring of Kalamos (see camping) to the **Bay of Aphales** with its clean shingle beach.

— Naturally there are satisfactory beaches for swimming at Kioni and Frikes, which villages have already been described.

Accommodation

The majority of Ithaka's modest hotel and pension capacity is at Vathi. The well-situated Mendor hotel, block-booked by Thompson until its recent withdrawal from Ithaka, will no doubt shortly feature in the brochure of some smaller tour operator.

Hotels on Ithaka

Class	Name	Rooms	Tel. (code 0674)
● At Vathi			
B	Mendor	36	32433
B	Odysseus (Pension)	10	32381
● At Frikes			
C	Nostos	27	31644

Villas Practically all are situated at Kioni, most of them on the books of Greek Islands Club of 66 High Street, Walton-on-Thames KT12 1BU and its associated flotilla sailing company.

Private rooms, on the other hand, are far more widely distributed, hardly a village being without at least a few. The largest numbers are at Vathi, Perachori, Kioni, Stavros and Frikes. In the smaller villages enquiries should be made at the café.

Camping There are no campsites on Ithaka. Summer campers make use of some shady foreshores on the north side of Vathi bay, where camping is tolerated by the authorities. Discreet camping is also possible in several directions beyond Stavros, where the countryside is generally much better wooded than in the south. There are two useful springs on the fringes of Platrithias (3kms north of Stavros); towards Exoghi is Melanidros, a medicinal water, which some say restored Homer his sight; and at the end of the road through Kolieri at Kalamos, where anyone who drinks the pure cold water that issues from its three spouts is assured of a future return to Ithaka.

These springs notwithstanding, there is actually a distinct water shortage in many parts of the island. Houses have traditionally depended on an ancient system of individual reservoirs called sternas to accumulate the winter rainfall, together with some communal wells put in by the Venetians. Both were considerably disrupted by the earthquake; so to meet the needs of the large transient summer population, water must often now be delivered by lorry. This must either be imported by ship, or produced from the desalination plant at Vathi, at a cost of more than £5 per cubic metre. Bottled drinking water can, of course, be bought relatively cheaply from most shops.

Products and the economy

In colonial times Ithaka was more than self-sufficient in agriculture. Wheat, wine, currants and olive oil were all exported, and as late as the end of the nineteenth century 31 windmills and 26 olive presses continued to function. The last sustained agricultural effort came during the second world war, when otherwise some islanders could well have starved. Most food now comes over from the mainland by ferry, much of it via Levkas and Astakos, since prices in Central Greece are cheaper than those of the Patras region of the Peloponnese.

Whilst depopulation continued, the falling harvest had to be balanced by remittances from emigrants, so many Ithakans continued to seek employment in shipping. This became easy after 1783, when the Russians compelled the Turks to give them rights of free passage through the Dardanelles, and Ithakan ships flying the Russian flag began to build up a substantial trade to the mouth of the Danube — a colony of Ithakans continues to reside in Roumania.

Although present day Ithaka produces little, it can at least offer work to its young people in the tourism and construction industries.

Restaurants are not sophisticated, but their food is reasonable in quality and price. Former specialities are becoming hard to find on the menus, but a sweet called *rovani,* made from rice, honey and olive oil, and distantly related to *baklava,* may still be encountered.

Homer's Ithaka

Helen, wife of Menelaus, King of Sparta, has eloped with Paris, son of the King of Troy. Menelaus appeals to his brother Agamemnon, High King of Mycenae, who orders preparations for a punitive expedition against Troy. Among those summoned by him is Odysseus, Lord of the Kefallenes, who brings twelve ships with him. The siege lasts for 10 years, until finally the Greeks manage to infiltrate by means of the Trojan Horse — a ruse devised by Odysseus himself. Troy falls, and the warriors set off on their return journey. The voyage of Odysseus is to last another ten years, during which he must overcome a daunting series of obstacles and misadventures. At last he comes to Ithaka, alone and in disguise, to be recognised only by his dog and his ancient nurse. He finds that in his absence his wife Penelope has been besieged by over one hundred suitors, clamouring ever more urgently for her to presume her husband dead and marry one of them. Helped by his son Telemachus and a few faithful servants, he kills their leaders and puts the rest to flight, once more to resume both his kingdom and his marriage-bed.

Such is the bare outline of the legend, but it can be no more than legend since we have no contemporary documents about it. Writing did exist, based on an immensely complex ideogram system of some 200 characters known as Linear B, which is not fully understood even today. But the many Linear B clay tablets to survive all seem to have been inventories, tax lists and the like — there is no evidence that this script was ever used for literature.

Classical tradition gives the historical date for the fall of Troy as 1184 BC — although various scholars have computed other dates between 1334 and 1127. Modern excavations at Troy itself reveal that the city was indeed destroyed after siege at about this time; and contemporary Hittite and Egyptian documents contain occasional names which may belong to people mentioned in the legend. Classical tradition continues, asserting that the Mycenaean dynasties participating in the siege themselves fell during the second generation after it, in the face of invasion from the north by the Dorians — another Greek-speaking tribe supposed to have been exiled descendants of the legendry hero Herakles (Hercules). Before long the Dorians took over most of the Mycenaean heartlands on the mainland of the Peloponnese, so displacing most of the previous rulers and their followers. Undoubtedly many descendants of those involved in the Trojan War eventually took refuge on the Aegean coast of Asia Minor and its offshore islands, in the region known as Ionia. And it was here, during the struggle to establish a new life on the fringe of the Greek-speaking world, that oral traditions of the 'good old days' were kept alive by itinerant story-tellers.

This period of Greek history, from the eleventh to ninth centuries BC, is known as the Dark Age — partly because so little of its detail remains to us. But elsewhere, in Cyprus and especially Phoenicia, more advanced societies of the day had succeeded in reducing the complicated Linear B writing system to practical new alphabetical scripts of fewer characters that almost anyone could learn to use. The Phoenicians employed the new writing for business purposes; but it was Greek poets and story-tellers who were magnificently to demonstrate its possibilities for literature. First and foremost among them stood Homer, who at some time around 800 BC wrote down definitively the legend of the Trojan Wars in his two vast epic poems, the *Iliad* and the *Odyssey*.

Literacy now fuelled the growth of the new Greek city-states, and within their intellectual ferment it was not long before questions began to be asked about the past. Who was this Homer, now claimed as a native son by so many cities? Could Homer himself have written both poems, in view of the stylistic differences between them? Why did some versions of the texts contain material, even entire episodes, not mentioned in others? These and other matters of authenticity became exciting intellectual hobby-horses for scholars — a process which reached its peak during the third century BC at the great library of the Ptolemies in Alexandria, where batteries of librarians were engaged in collecting, copying, classifing and criticising all the available manuscripts — many of them now lost to us.

Not until the rise of the middle classes in northern Europe during the seventeenth and eighteenth centuries was the Homeric legacy again so powerfully to grip the collective imagination of society. Soon no gentleman could call himself educated who had not read his *Iliad* and *Odyssey*, preferably from the original Greek. Antagonisms of language and style, inconsistencies in narrative, and conflicts of geography were eagerly argued in learned journals. In time the most intriguing of these puzzles came to be known as the 'Ithaka Question'.

The problem arises from the many detailed geographical descriptions in the poems, and the impossibility of reconciling spacial relationships between Homer's Ithaka, Doulichon (perhaps Levkas), Skheria (perhaps Corfu), the Echinai and elsewhere, with the actual position of Ithaka today. Explanation would be easier were Homer's Ithaka some other island; and one must not forget that when an entire population had to abandon an island, use of the old name sometimes continued for the new one — as happened over Aegean Alonissos, for example. This was a favourite type of hypothesis, and Corfu, Paxi, Levkas, and a part of Kefallonia were variously proposed as Homer's Ithaka; alternatively that it had simply vanished beneath the sea. Textual analysis alone was soon seen to be inadequate; and in an age of reason it seemed self-evident that scientific archeology must become the tool to resolve matters. Seventeenth century investigations had suggested two sites on Ithaka itself as possible locations for the city of Odysseus, and in 1806 two British archeologists began digging there — Sir William Gell at Aetos in the south, and Colonel Leake at Pelikata in the north.

A local poet, drawing inspiration from Homer, has enshrined his own words on a plaque he has erected beside the spring of Kalamos.

Welcome stranger to Kalamos well.
Bend and drink from your cupped hand its ice cold water.
Breathe in around you the holy fragrance,
And you shall return again to Ithaka.

Whilst their own diggings revealed little, and had to be interrupted suddenly when the French took over the island, both gentlemen exercised their imaginations to good effect to discover and name various bays, fountains, caves and other features whose topography seemed appropriate to the locations described by Homer — names that remain associated, however dubious their basis, even to the present day. Others followed in their footsteps — even the great Schliemann himself, to Aetos in 1867 on the first of his many Greek forays — but little of positive value was revealed.

Nor have a number of twentieth-century investigations provided conclusive proofs, though they have altered the balance of probabilities. Any Homeric correlation, to be convincing, must demonstrate traces of late Mycenaean occupation. Nothing suitable has been found on Corfu or Paxos; Levkas has been inconclusive, in spite of sustained efforts there; but Kefallonia at least gave many indications of such communities. On Ithaka itself the Aetos site was linked to a town called Alalkomenes, which seems to have been founded several centuries too late, although fourth and third century coins were discovered there, bearing a face considered to be that of Ulysses.

The Pelikata ridge above Stavros, on the other hand, demonstrated continuous occupation between 2200 and 1200 BC, with some evidence of a Mycenaean palace at the summit. Moreover in a cave sanctuary below in the bay of Polis were found terracotta masks of about the first century BC, one of them inscribed 'my vow to Odysseus'. Even more significant were fragments from twelve bronze Geometric tripod vases dating from about the ninth century BC. Homer relates that Odysseus brought thirteen such tripods back with him, and hid them in a cave near his landing-place on Ithaka. Local gossip intriguingly has it that a thirteenth tripod was found there some years previously!

In further support of Pelicata as the city of Odysseus are Homer's descriptions 'between three mountains' and with 'views of three seas' Mounts Neritos, Exoghis and Marmakas, and the bays of Frikes, Aphales and the channel to the west appear to fit these admirably.

Today it seems increasingly futile to strive to reconcile the textual inconsistencies. Our experience with other ancient documents, even the Bible itself, has shown what errors and distortions can accrue to them with the passage of time. It also seems increasingly likely that personages and events from several generations of Mycenaean excursion may have found themselves telescoped into the one Homeric saga. Perhaps we should relax, secure in the belief that there is probably no candidate for Ithaka better than Ithaka itself? For in matters of the imagination belief is in any case more potent than truth.

Homer is a hard act to follow so let another poet have the last word! Konstantinos Kavafis (or Cafavy) (1863-1933) was a poet with a mission to reinterpret the Greek classical period for his own times. These are some fragments from his long poem about Ithaka:

> 'When you set out on the voyage to Ithaca,
> Pray that your journey may be long,
> Full of adventures, full of knowledge.
> Do not by any means hasten your voyage,
> Let it best endure for many a year,
>
> ...
>
> Ithaca gave you your splendid journey,
> Without her you would not have set out.
> Now she has nothing left to offer.
> You who have grown so wise, with so much experience,
> Will surely have realised just what Ithaca means?'

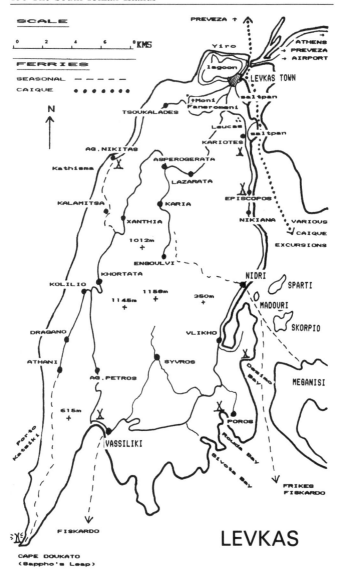

SCALE

0   2   4   6   8 KMS

FERRIES

SEASONAL   — — — —

CAIQUE   • • • • • • •

N

PREVEZA

Yiro

lagoon

ATHENS
PREVEZA
AIRPORT

LEVKAS TOWN

saltpan

Moni
Faneromani

Leucas

TSOUKALADES

saltpan

KARIOTES

AG. NIKITAS

ASPEROGERATA

EPISCOPOS

Kathisma

LAZARATA

KALAMITSA

KARIA

NIKIANA

VARIOUS

XANTHIA

CAIQUE
EXCURSIONS

1012m
+

ENGOULVI

KHORTATA

NIDRI

SPARTI

KOLILIO

1150m
+

350m
+

MADOURI

1145m
+

SKORPIO

DRAGANO

VLIKHO

ATHANI

SYVROS

MEGANISI

AG. PETROS

Desino Bay

615m
+

POROS

VASSILIKI

Rouda Bay

Sivota Bay

FRIKES
FISKARDO

Porto
Katsiki

FISKARDO

LEVKAS

CAPE DOUKATO
(Sappho's Leap)

TWELVE

Levkas

Population: 19,947   Highest Point: 1,158m
Area: 303 sq km   Hotel beds: 842

Levkas (Levkada, Levkados) takes its name from its white cliffs in the extreme south of the island. It is without doubt the 'odd one out' among the islands covered by this book. For whilst Kefallonia, Ithaka and Zakynthos have their own quite distinctive features, they are unified by their geography and geology and, in consequence, by their history and the common effects this has had on customs, architecture and landscape. From all three of them, as indeed from all the other islands of the Ionian, Levkas is quite different.

To begin with, its very status as an island is ambiguous. Were it not for the works of man, and in particular the shipping canal carefully dredged around its north-east corner, very probably it would find itself still joined to the mainland of Akarnania. Even today this channel narrows at its most crossable point to a thread of water less than 50m wide — a barrier of puny significance to any military force in control of the mainland.

Yet another difference is due to geology, demonstrated in spectacular manner by the fault lines between tectonic plates, the movement of which causes earthquakes. The main fault line in the area runs west from the Gulf of Corinth between Zakynthos and Kefallonia, and was responsible for the severe earthquakes there and on Ithaka in 1953. Levkas, on the other hand, comes at the end of another fault line running south from Yugoslavia through the mountains of North and Central Greece. So far as Levkas is concerned, earthquakes tend to be more frequent but less severe — the last serious one was in 1948.

Proximity to the mainland combined with the height of its mountains and the cliffs which extend down most of the west coast have also resulted in greater extremes of microclimate. Thus the west and parts of the south tend to be windy, sometimes very windy indeed, whereas the sheltered east coast is usually quite calm.

Levkas is the most densely populated of the four islands, in relation to its potential for cultivation. Rather than emigrate, the people have tended to follow the route of agricultural self-sufficiency, skilfully terracing their steep hillsides and by careful husbandry making the most of all the circumstances with which nature provided them. In this they received little help over the centuries from their nominal rulers. Because of its situation and the lack of a proper port, Levkas never fitted conveniently into the transport framework of the other islands; even overland communication remained problematical until relatively recently. Out of sight and partly out of mind it continued to subsist amidst some considerable poverty, until during the past two decades its unspoiled and unsophisticated charm started to become known to the wider world. When tourism arrived it fortunately dispersed itself between a number of centres — Levkas town, Nidri, Vasiliki and even smaller villages. Profits when they came were ploughed back into improved buildings and facilities; but as yet there has been little damage to the qualities which make the island attractive. And whilst it remains the poorest in the Ionian, a new prosperity is beginning to diffuse quite widely among the people,

Levkas administers one of the four *nomes* into which the Ionian islands are divided for purposes of local government, which includes the substantial islands of Meganisi, Kalamos and Kastos, in addition to a number of smaller islands.

Arrival by road

It is convenient to begin a discussion of how to get to Levkas with a description of the local mainland road network. Not that many readers will be driving there; but it is helpful to have an understanding of the roads before coming on to more normal means of holiday travel.

The road arrangement is dominated not only by mountains, but more importantly by the Ambracian gulf (or Bay of Amvrakikos), an expanse of enclosed sea-water so vast that under most circumstances it is preferable to wait to cross its narrow entrance on the ferry rather than drive round it. This is the route from Preveza in the north, the most important town in the region, whose ferry runs quite frequently and inexpensively all day and night across to

Aktion (see page 34). After passing the airport of Preveza (Aktion) after 2kms, a modern road diverges to the south and the small village of Ag. Nikolaos, where it joins the other main route from the south and east. From Athens or Patras, for example, one can take the 5/E19 main highway to the north west through Agrinion, leaving it at Amfilochia for the 42 towards Aktion. A shorter and quieter alternative leaves the main highway at Missolonghi for the new coastal road through Astakos, which joins the earlier route at the large straggling village of Vonitsa. At the entrance to the village a sharp left turning doubles back towards Ag. Nikolaos and Levkas; at the far end a T-junction joins the main road from Amfilochia, which continues to skirt the gulf, past the airport to the ferry.

The final stage beyond Ag. Nikolaos crosses low-lying salt-marshes, and the tarmac comes to a temporary halt at Fort St Mauro, one of a half dozen forts in the vicinity built to control the strategic approaches to Levkas, in particular the shipping canal which passes under its battlements. The boat ferry across this narrow channel was long ago replaced by a chain ferry, more recently duplicated by a second chain ferry. Even so, long queues of vehicles used sometimes to build up in summer, and as a result the chain ferries lie rusting in the shadow of a fine new pontoon bridge which now straddles the gap. This has facilities for rapidly lifting either or both ramps connecting it to the shore, to allow smaller craft to pass; or more laboriously to crank itself round and lie alongside the bank, thus opening sufficient width of channel for larger ships. The bridge will open up, if so required, every hour on the hour during daylight hours. The bridge-builders have painted the words *F/B Ag. Mavra* on this structure; but whether that is an example of sardonic Greek humour, or a subterfuge to qualify for government shipbuilding subsidy is uncertain!

Once across the bridge you need to turn left to approach the town along a 1km causeway between the shipping canal and a large shallow lagoon; it would be possible to reach it too by a 10km detour, skirting the lagoon by a surfaced road which runs the length of its enclosing sand-bank — known as the Yiro.

A number of buses go across from Levkas to the mainland. Four leave each day for Athens via Agrinion, a journey that nowadays takes only 6 hours. Another four go towards Preveza, as far as the Aktion ferry, passing the airport on the way; the bus does not continue on to the ferry, so if you need to go to Preveza itself you must travel as a foot passenger; from the Preveza side it would be a further km walk to the bus terminal there, for Parga or

Igoumenitsa. Finally, a number of the scheduled flights arriving at the airport are met by a KTEL bus from Levkas — as well as the Olympic Airways bus to Preveza, which does take the ferry.

In addition to a number of taxis in Levkas town, there are usually two or three waiting on the Aktion side of the ferry, as well as at the airport when flights are expected.

The internal road system for getting about the island will be discussed in more detail below. For present purposes it is sufficient that a satisfactory ring-road out of Levkas town encircles the island, linking all the tourist villages and both the car ferry ports, and that buses connect the capital with all of them between three and nine times each day.

Arrival by air

The airport of Preveza (Aktion) is situated at a distance of 19kms from Levkas town, which in summer is the ultimate destination of many passengers.

Scheduled There are no international flights. There is about one daily Olympic Airways flight from Athens airport (west) by Short 330 or the tiny Dornier 228, duration 1hr 20mins. Most of these flights are met by the KTEL bus from Levkas (see above). Scorpio Travel, on the first floor of a conspicuous building at the entrance to the main street in Levkas town, is the agent for Oympic Airways.

Charter In 1988 there were up to 14 charter flights weekly, about half of them from the UK (Gatwick and Manchester). This is projected to increase in future years. Seat only passengers will probably not be covered by the tour operator's insurance for travel on his airport coaches, and so will be unable legally to make use of them. But taxis or public buses should be available at reasonable cost, as above.

The civil terminal is a small but adequate concrete structure on the north side of the airfield. The airport is shared with the military, whose installations are on the other side. Naturally it is forbidden to take photos.

(Opposite) *Vassiliki Bay (Levkas). The bright colourful coastline of the southeast and east of the island, pleasure ground for tourism, contrasts with the inhospitable west coast (see next page).*

Arrival by sea

The most direct route from abroad is the summer service by Hellenic Cruising Holidays from Brindisi to Preveza, for which Scorpio Travel is the Levkas agent. You could also take the ferry operated by Seven Islands Travel to either Vathi or Sami, and then one of the ongoing ferries to Vassiliki or Nidri (see below). It is also possible to take any ferry to Patras, and continue on to Levkas by bus (some of the Athens buses to Levkas go via Patras, the others can be picked up at Andirrion — see Chapter 14). Details of all these services are listed in Chapter 3.

Locally there are direct car ferry services from Kefallonia and Ithaka to small ports in Levkas, both operated by open deck car ferries. One, based in Sami (Kefallonia), crosses from Fiskardo to **Vassiliki**. The other operates a triangular route to **Nidri** from Fiskardo (Kefallonia) and Frikes (Ithaka).

In the past there were spasmodic attempts to establish an occasional direct summer ferry link between Nidri and Patras; but with the improving bus service this seems to have been abandoned.

Summary of ferries

● From Italy.
— Brindisi/Preveza. 3 x weekly July-Aug +. 18 hrs. *M/V Remvi.*
— Brindisi/Ithaka or Kefallonia. 3 x weekly June & Sept, daily July & Aug. 16hrs. Fares: pax. from 5000drs, cars from 5500drs. *C/F Ionis, C/F Ionian Glory.*
● Local.
— Fiskardo/Vassiliki. 2 x daily June-Sept. 1hr. Fares: pax. 319drs, car 1320drs. *C/F Aphrodite L.*
— Fiskardo and Frikes/Nidri. 2 x daily April to Sept, 2 x 3 days a week in Oct. 1½hrs +. Fares: pax. 371drs, cars 2041drs. *C/F Meganisi, C/F Levkas.*

Levkas town

It is entirely fitting that this unconventional island should have such an unusual capital. Levkas town may perhaps seem reminiscent of one of those half-forgotten little fishing towns in the Po delta of

(Opposite) *Human sacrifices were made to Apollo and other gods at the temple which once stood just above this modern lighthouse at 'Sappho's Leap' (see page 173).*

The yacht berths in Levkas town, in process of development towards a full-scale marina. The KTEL bus station is situated to the left, opposite.

Italy, but it certainly has little in common with other Ionian towns or indeed with the rest of the island. Until the end of the nineteenth century it was known as Amaxikhi, most likely because of the many donkey carts *(amaxa)* found loading and unloading there. Earlier travellers described it variously as wretched, ill-built and unclean. Of course much real improvement has taken place since then; but in any event today's travellers, too much conditioned to modern uniformities in concrete, are more likely to find considerable charm in the curiosities of its layout, the uniquely indigenous style of its buildings, and the lively individuality of its inhabitants.

The houses themselves are certainly remarkable. Whilst ground floors appear conventional enough, from the outside at least, upper levels are clad with a variety of temporary-looking sheeting materials. This makes sense only when you realise that corrugated metal, external-grade hardboard sheeting and clapboard are the modern equivalent of the light-weight plaster and reed screens traditionally chosen as being less vulnerable during an earthquake. The custom is maintained even in modern houses, regardless of their reinforced concrete framework; whilst older buildings have been strengthened inside by secondary frameworks of timber, intended to prevent the upper parts from falling in on their occupants. Bright pastel shades of fresh paint lend an atmosphere of stylish good taste to these eccentric buildings.

The town is fortunate that its ad-hoc appeal came to be appreciated before too much pressure for modernisation built up. It is fortunate also to be surrounded by plenty of land, existing or easily reclaimed, and to have administrators with vision and energy to devise an intelligent and sensitive development plan, now being implemented. Already a broad lozenge of ring road is in place, shielding the older parts of the town from excessive traffic, and defining an area where conservation has some priority.

Orientation is not immediately obvious on your first arrival. You come across the causeway to find yourself at the top right-hand corner of the lozenge. To your left is a green area of **public park** and playground, flanked by various modern buildings hotels, travel agents, motor hire firms etc. The ring road runs between these and the 'deep-water' part of the quayside, before bearing right past a long line of shallower yacht berths. At this point no doubt the development plan makes provision for a relief road for through traffic on its way to the east coast. At present, older patterns persist, and the ring road soon reaches a zone where streams of traffic converge from a number of directions — it is as well that a policeman is usually on duty to sort out the confusion.

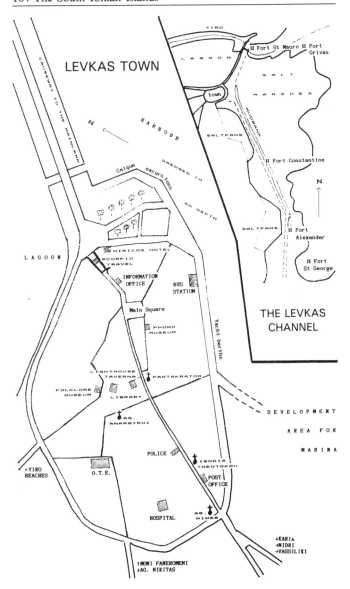

LEVKAS TOWN

VIRO

LAGOON

☩ Fort St Mauro ☩ Fort Grivas

SALT

MARSHES

town

N

HARBOUR

SALTPANS

MUDBANK

DREDGED TO

Calque excursions

5m DEPTH

☩ Fort Constantine

N

LAGOON

SALTPANS

☩ Fort Alexander

NIRICOS HOTEL

SCORPIO TRAVEL

INFORMATION OFFICE

BUS STATION

☩ Fort St George

Main Square

PHONO MUSEUM

Yacht berths

THE LEVKAS CHANNEL

LIGHTHOUSE TAVERNA

FOLKLORE MUSEUM

LIBRARY

☩ PANTAKRATOR

☩ AG. ANARGYROI

DEVELOPMENT

AREA FOR

MARINA

POLICE

☩ ISODIA THEOTOKOU

←YIRO BEACHES

O.T.E.

POST OFFICE

HOSPITAL

☩ AG. MINAS

↓KARIA
→NIDRI
→VASSILIKI

☩MONI FANERONENI
↓AG. NIKITAS

Back at the entrance to the town, the ring road continues to the right along the lagoon, to give eventual access to various parts of the north west of the island. Just ahead of you a couple of inconspicuous narrow lanes are in fact the beginning of the town's **main street;** it doesn't matter which one you take because they soon converge before arriving at the central square; the main street then continues diagonally through the town, emerging at the traffic policeman.

In addition to improving the road network, changes affecting several important buildings are being made. Already the KTEL **bus station,** formerly a major contributor to the zone of confusion, has relocated opposite the yacht berths. A process of renovating other important buildings is under way; one of the two banks is about to make a move from the square, the Town Hall staff are already occupying temporary premises, and further changes will follow. No commercially produced town map could keep pace with such momentum, so it is just as well that one of the renovated buildings, on the way to the central square, is due to open its doors in 1989 as a brand-new municipal information office.

You can stand in the **central square** in the evening and listen as the strains of Boccherini or Souza float out from the practice rooms of the Philharmonica Levkada (established 1850) — or, if you are lucky, you can even watch the band perform, dressed in full uniform, in the square itself. Around you the local people swirl past on their *volta,* freshly washed and dressed, parading up and down the main street, which has its own atmosphere, in part imported from some oriental bazaar. At every hand there are opportunities for eating and drinking, interspersed with the display of local products; artisan's cooperatives sell dolls, weaving, embroidery, metal-work and pottery; there are wine shops, and stalls with many kinds of locally made food — honey, *mandolato* (nougat), yogourt and salami among them. Before long it is all to be repaved and pedestrianised. Let us hope that the new elegance will not draw in too many more chic boutiques and consumer durable stores, to drive out the little shops and so upset the long-evolved pattern of work-a-day trading which has, after all, given the street its character.

Another main street attraction is the facades of several **churches** — some of their names are marked on the map. These have been rebuilt a number of times after earthquakes, but they do give some idea of the local styles of the seventeenth and eighteenth centuries. At the far end of the street Ag. Minas suffered the misfortune to be gutted by fire, and the more recent indignity of burglary. The police station, only five blocks away, just off the main street, now incorporates the tourist police, but your chance of a meaningful exchange would probably depend on whether some other visitor to the station could translate for you — better to go to the new information office instead.

There are no fewer than four museums in the town, all of them free, though a small tip may be appropriate. The most important of them is the **Art Gallery** on the ground floor of the public library building — a librarian will open it up and show you around. A number of the earlier paintings and icons in this well-displayed collection are in a transitional style evidently grounded on the Byzantine, but showing a marked Renaissance influence. Open every morning and most evenings except Sunday. The **Archeological Museum** is situated rather remotely in a modern building on the road towards Faneromeni. The staff will probably be surprised that you have taken the trouble to come, for whilst it contains objects discovered by Dörpfeld, and includes some fascinating photos of his excavations, few visitors find their way here. Open mornings except Tuesdays. More convenient to most visitors will be the **Folklore Museum,** where some upstairs rooms contain an engaging display of bygone costumes, furniture and other artifacts. Finally, just off the back of the main square in Kalikani is the so-called **Phonographic Museum.** This does indeed contain some sound recordings, among other items assembled to remind us of Levkas in times gone by. Open daily (in season) 0900-1300 and 1800-2300. Next door is the shop of Mr Nikis Katopodis, who stocks books in several languages, all of which he speaks; he is also a noted photographer.

Getting something to eat in the town is never a problem. *Souvlaki,* various meat, cheese and vegetable pies and other fast food can be bought at several stalls in the main street. Opposite the Pantokrator church (the one with the clock tower beside it) and just off the main street, the Lighthouse taverna is a restaurant well-suited to foreigners, because of the warm welcome they get from its owner Steve Ventouras, who worked in America for some years. Steve will serve you, inside or out in the garden, whilst his wife Georgia prepares delicious traditional Greek dishes. The taverna most highly regarded by local people is the Adriatica, also with garden, out on the road towards Faneromeni.

An evening can be finished off in one of the three cinemas, two of which screen outdoors in season. Any holiday ills could probably be soothed away at the Levkada Physiotherapy Centre in the main street, which offers sauna and massage treatment. Otherwise there are two chemist shops in the main street, and a small hospital near the OTE building.

Indigenous architecture in Levkas town. Note the corrugated and tile roof, a light timber-framed upper storey filled in with plaster, the elegant wrought-iron balcony, substantial walls at street level, and an entrance slightly raised as a precaution against flooding.

Getting about

Before setting forth it would be best to take a look at how to get out and about, beyond the town.

Buses The new KTEL bus terminal is situated in a building near the north end of the yacht berths. A large board inside lists the timings of services, which vary according to season. Most villages receive two ro three daily services all the year, though the first of them usually leaves at crack of dawn. More important villages, such as Nidri and Karia, have higher frequencies. Circular services round the ring road, pausing at Vassiliki for a few hours, are usually scheduled in summer. There are two windows for buying tickets — *Athenon* for the Athens service and *Topikon* (local) for the rest.

Taxis There are about 50 in all, most of them in the town, at either end of the main street or beside the square. Others are based on Nikiana, Nidri and Vassiliki.

Vehicle hire Cars, mopeds and bicycles can be hired in the town. Aravanis, beyond the Levkas Hotel, has a responsible attitude and speaks good English. His rates are typical, and in 1988 were:

Jeep or Fiat Ritmo	6000drs per day
Motorbike, 175cc or 250cc	3000 or 3500drs per day
Scooter (Vespa, Honda or Yamaha)	1500drs per day

Terms: 10% discount weekly, 20% discount monthly.

Bicycles are perfectly suitable for short excursions from the town.

Caiques The town's four travel agents run caique trips from the town. These leave at about 0900 (and sometimes in early evening) from the deep-water berths near the public park, where boards display details of forthcoming excursions; these can vary between a beach party and a long day-trip to other islands, even as far as Kefallonia. The travel agents are also pleased to arrange your vehicle hire requirements.

Maps At least two different editions are available. The status of the road network is more accurately shown on the Tourist map of Levkada (Voukelatos); it covers a wider area, including even the trips of Kefallonia and Ithaka, with a plan of Levkas town on the back. Levkada (Toubi's) has the larger map of Levkas itself, with rather more written information on the back.

Tour of the island

The main road round the island, marked with a thick line on the map, passes through or near every village of tourist interest, other than some parts of the west coast which are described separately. Petrol stations are fairly plentiful in the east and south; but be warned that there are none on the 29km section to the west between Lazarata and Vassiliki.

To join the island ring in a clockwise direction, follow the signposts to Nidri on the outskirts of Levkas town. After 3km and a sharp right turn southwards at Kalligoni, you can pause below the hillside on which the Corinthians founded their colony of **Leucas** (also known as Nerikos). This you can climb without much difficulty, to find a section of the ancient wall in good condition.

This is a good vantage point for looking out over the shipping channel, and pondering the peculiar topography between Levkas and the mainland, and the tides of history that have ebbed and flowed around it. The seventh century Corinthians were the first historical figures to leave their imprint. In addition to the city under your feet, it was they who dug the original canal, to save their trading ships the long and sometimes dangerous passage round the southern cape. By the time of the Peloponnesian War the canal seems to have silted up, or maybe the levels altered, since ships had to be dragged across the isthmus. If so it was certainly restored by the Romans, and has been in use ever since. The Byzantines extended the city walls, and there are some remains of their fort on the ridge behind you. At the beginning of the fourteenth century, a hundred years after the island was lost to Byzantium, the Frankish ruler of the day built the first Fort St Mauro (which can be visited — the key is held in a nearby café). Before long Fort St George was also put up to keep an eye on the southern approaches. Control oscillated between Venetian Christian and Ottoman infidel, both of whom extensively remodelled the defences to accord with the latest technology. Further fortifications were added during the confusing period of the French revolution, first by the treacherous and ambitious Ali Pasha of Ioannina, who staked his own claim by putting up the castle of Grivas (Frourio Tekes). This led the Russians during their short-lived protectorate to counter with Forts Alexander and Constantine, built in mid-channel. Fort St Mauro was captured from the French by the British in 1810 — and after that, Levkas was no longer in the front line.

The deep shipping canal was first dredged by the British. It was realigned in 1905, to its present depth of 5m. Below to the right you can see a large expanse of saltpans *(alikes),* which are still in active production, unlike the similar ones nearer the town which are fit only for redevelopment.

The road continues south past increasingly pleasant small hamlets, Kariotes, Episkopos and Nikiana amongst them, until arriving at the superbly situated **Nidri**. The village is protected and sheltered on all sides. Behind it a ring of mountains encloses fertile valleys and slopes planted with citrus orchards and olive groves. To seaward lie the calm waters of the bay of Vlikho, and the scattering of islands beyond; tree-girt Madouri, austere Sparti, Skorpio of the Onassis clan, and steep Meganisi, hidden from the village by the sheltering arm of the Ag. Kiriaki peninsula; these islands and the ferry will be discussed under Meganisi below.

Nidri is well used to foreigners and their curious ways. At the end of the last century it devoted itself to the great Dörpfeld, who had started his archeological career as assistant to the even greater Schliemann. Dörpfeld was convinced that Levkas, not Ithaka, corresponded to Homer's Ithaka, and so consequently he spent half his life here, digging behind Nidri and elsewhere on the island to try and prove his argument. His finds, though of great interest, are now generally thought not to have coincided sufficiently with the Late Mycenaean period to make his case. But such was his fame that the Kaiser sent a pre-fabricated house, which was erected on the end of the Ag. Kiriaki peninsula, for him to live in. Unfortunately it burnt down in 1980; you can see his monument — the Mnimion Dörpfeld — whose column supports a nymph; and his grave can be found beneath a stone near his house.

Today's village has been equally happy to surrender itself to the new tourists, who have gladly accepted their freedom of the village. The freemen swarm up and down a main street bursting with travel offices, car-hire firms, souvenir shops, boutiques, cafés, restaurants, discos and cinemas — whilst brightly-blazered company reps flash to and fro among them. For this is package-holiday territory, where sailing flotillas, schools for windsurfing, villas and village rooms are all efficiently dispensed by foreign tour operators. If an independent traveller, you will need local help, and would be well advised to talk to someone like Mr Damianos Gazis of Nidri Travel, who will gladly fix you up with accommodation, transport (car, moped or bicycle), and a free map of walks in the countryside behind the village. Bill and Pauline of The Taste of Greece would also be pleased to give you the benefit of their friendly advice.

Vlikho itself, at the head of the creek, is of no great interest unless to glance at its boatyards, where caiques are built and repaired. But the south of Levkas, between here and Vassiliki, is as delightful as any part of the island, and contains some of the best campsites (see below). A short detour to **Poros,** a substantial village perched high above the coast, gives the opportunity to inspect the ruins of a fourth-century BC tower beyond it, or to enjoy the bathing facilities at Rouda bay far below. An inland detour through the mountain village of **Syvros,** emerging near Vassiliki, is also rewarding. Otherwise you should not fail to make a short diversion, your camera at the ready, to the bay of **Sivota,** approached down a narrow valley through groves of ancient gnarled olive trees. The inlet is deservedly popular with yachtsmen, not only for its superbly sheltered anchorage, but for the present rustic simplicity of the tiny hamlet; Stavros and his daughter Voula will give you a warm welcome at the Restaurant Stavros, one of the two tavernas.

Vassiliki is a much larger village which has succeeded in absorbing substantial tourist development whilst continuing to retain the genuine character of a small fishing port. The 'ordinary' visitors find all they need for a simple holiday — shops, cafés, tavernas,

Waterside scene at the fishing port of Vassiliki.

discos, scooter hire, and a vast bathing beach. The twice-daily ferry to Fiskardo (Kefallonia) is also an attraction. But above all it is a mecca for windsurfers, who are drawn by the regular rythm of the wind cycle — early morning *piano,* midday *crescendo,* afternoon *forte.* There is an advanced windsurfing school at Ponti on the far side of the bay — conditions are rather too demanding for novices — and special-interest holidays here are regularly featured in the windsurfing press.

The return to Levkas town begins with a steep climb up into the mountain to Ag. Petros, and continues to wind its scenic way at high altitude past poor but picturesque villages — Khortata, Xanthia, Asperogerata — until it turns away from the sea to descend into a more fertile area of upland valleys. At the end of the seventeenth century this part was settled by the Venetians with some of their former subjects from Crete — an island they had recently lost to the Turks. **Karia,** the chief village, redolent of centuries of industrious husbandry, is well worth the short diversion. It is large and rambling, poised high on a hillside overlooking the green circular bowl of the Livadi — formerly overwintering quarters for flocks of sheep brought down from their mountainous summer grazings. Much of the island's lace is made here, and some marvellous examples are displayed in village shops. Roadbuilding continues apace in this area, but whilst the drive down to Nidri is both panoramic and exhilarating, for the present it is better done in someone else's vehicle!

The main road returns through Lazarata, pausing for a spectacular view across the lagoon and its encircling barrier before plunging into a long series of zig-zags down to town.

Cape Doukato and 'Sappho's Leap'

An excursion to the southern extremity of the island is not something to be attempted lightly. Already 50kms from Levkas town, the narrowness and rough condition of the final section of road make it seem even further. And should you wish to linger over the trip, the problem of where or how to spend the night may arise. Nevertheless in good weather and with suitable transport this excursion is as rewarding as anything that Levkas can offer.

You leave the ring road a couple of kilometres south of Khortata, to follow a signpost to Komilio; then continue through Dragano, still high up the side of the mountainous ridge, to **Athani.** Thus far the road, though narrow and sometimes twisting, has been more or less surfaced, but do not be misled: pause, and take this last opportunity to refresh yourself, however humbly — the wine at least is as good as any in the island — before setting out on the last lonely 15kms. This should, ideally, be accomplished in a hired Jeep, especially if you intend to plunge down one of the so-called 'tracks' leading to those astonishing sandy beaches that will so tantalise you from high above; alternatively bring your own sturdy motor-caravan, driven at walking pace over the undulating humps of rock, in which you can later (as I did) pass the night.

At the far end is the modern lighthouse, which you may well have already remarked from the Patras ferry. Above it, so Strabo tells us, was once a temple to Apollo, from whose religious observances the 'Leap' derived. No doubt it started as a sacrifice, when some criminal or mental-defective was pushed off to propitiate the god. Perhaps occasionally some wretched victim was lucky enough to survive? Thus it seems to have developed into a ritual of trial, and still later an entertainment, when live birds were attached to brake the descent, and the outcome was awaited by rescue boats below. That much seems established — although one wonders today how any large crowd of spectators managed to get themselves to such an inaccessible spot. But its association with Sappho seems based on nothing but ill-digested myth.

The lady herself was real enough. She had the good fortune to be born on Lesbos, at a time during the sixth century BC when that island was ruled by a group of aristocratic families to which she herself belonged. Cultured people of both sexes wrote poems almost as letters to one another. Sappho — a married woman with her own daughter — was so accomplished in the arts that young girls were sent from all over Ionia to study at what was, in modern terms, her 'finishing school'. Naturally when pupils left, it fell to Sappho to write some commemorative lyrics; if they were leaving to be married or to join another teacher, she was not a woman to try and disguise her passionate regrets. But it was for a later, crude and male-chauvinistic generation to fabricate the web of scandal and perversion that has tarnished her reputation ever since. 'Sappho in love' became a stock figure of caricature, one playwright going so far as to provide her with two fellow-poets as paramours — one who was probably dead before she was born, the other probably not yet born when she died!

Poor Sappho! Nor did the good times last out her own lifetime. The people rioted against the aristocrats, electing her enemy Pittakos as tyrant, so she and others of her sort had to leave Lesbos. She seems to have visited Sicily; she may even have joined her friend and fellow poet Alkaios in Egypt; but there is no record that she ever went to Levkas, much less that unrequited love of any kind impelled her to leap to her death from Cape Doukato. It is sad too that she lives for most of us only as the 'burning Sappho' of Byron's Isles of Greece, rather than through her own lyrics, whose Aiolic forms and rustic dialect, like some delicate island that does not 'travel', have defied the best attempts at satisfactory translation.

Ag. Nikitas

The north west corner of the island must be reached by yet another road out of Levkas town, which climbs into the hills past the monastery of **Faneromeni.** Many Greeks come to pay their devotions here, but tourists are more likely to pause only for a view — for the building itself is modern. So too is the final section of the road beyond Tsoukalades, which has quite suddenly opened up the nearest of those magnificent but often inaccessible sand and shingle beaches that extend the entire length of the western coastline. The village was once a simple cluster of houses sheltering from the wind on a hillside at the far end of the vast beach. The villagers seem as surprised as any at the changes now taking place to their former fishing community. The next beach at Kathisma has also become accessible, as creeping development advances. By road it is no longer difficult to continue directly to the south, joining the main road beyond Kalamitsa.

Beaches

The island's beaches can hold their own with any in the Ionian. Some have already had brief mention, others will emerge under Camping, whilst the better-known ones are indicated on the island map. Composition does not vary too much from a mixture of coarse sand and fine shingle, though the east coast tends to be more pebbly. Your choice will probably depend on the day's need for shelter from sun and wind; your means of transport, and the time and energy at your disposal; and the facilities — such as places to

The village and beach of Ag. Nikitas

eat and watersports. The latter have as yet been rather un-sophisticated except in the area of windsurfing, but that could change quite quickly; your nearest travel office will be able to tell you the present position.

Accommodation

Hotels
Most of the larger hotels have been built quite recently. One of the longer-established ones is the Niricos, whose bedrooms look out over the causeway towards St Mauro. This family hotel, which remains open all the year, seems to provide a better combination of local atmosphere and value for money than the nearby Levkas and Xenia.

The Gallini, 13kms to the south, is well situated both for a quiet family holiday and to take advantage of what delights Levkas town or nearby Nidri have to offer. The hotel provides a spacious high quality bungalow complex pleasantly situated above a private beach with facilities for windsurfing and pottering about in small boats.

Hotels on Levkas

Class	Name	Rooms	Tel. (code 0645)
● In Levkas town			
B	Apollon	34	31122
B	Levkas	93	23916
B	Xenia Levkas	64	24762
C	Niricos	36	24132
C	Santa Mavra	23	22342
and 3 lower category hotels.			
● At or near Nikiana			
B	Alexandros	27	71376
	Galini (Apartments)	20	92431
● At Nidri			
B	Nidrio Akti (Pension)	16	92400
and one lower category hotel.			
● At Vassiliki			
C	Levkatas	33	31305
and one lower category hotel.			

Villas and rooms
Private rooms are available in all parts of the island, with the greatest concentration naturally in the capital, and near the tourist villages in the east and south coasts, where there are also a few villas and apartments for rent.

Camping
Levkas makes good provision for campers, as it also does for visiting yachtsmen. There is a varied selection of campsites, most of them with plenty of trees for shade and adequate facilities including power-points. In order of distance from the town, they are:
— **Camping Kariotes Beach** (3kms). Satisfactory for a short stay, perhaps. Open 15 May—end Sept.
— **Camping Episkopos Beach** (8kms), between Katouna and Nikiana. A larger and better organised site, adjoining the landward side of the coast road. Open June to Sept.
— **Camping Ag. Nikiti** (11kms) at Ag. Nikitas. Not an 'official' site, and at present little more than an open field. But police recognise it, so it remains the only place on the east coast where you can legally pitch.
— **Camping Desimo** (21kms). A small high-quality site with private beach well suited for water sports beside Desimi bay, which is approached from the road round Vlichos bay. It is invariably full in summer, but a second site is due to open there in 1989. Open May to Oct.
— **Camping Poros Beach** (31kms). At present the largest camping area in Levkas, situated in Rouda bay below Paros. Actually two sites, the smaller one organised by the Poros Community, open from April to October; the larger privately owned, including some 20 bungalows for rent, open from June to mid-Sept. A delightful situation if you don't mind the isolation — which is mitigated by a good-sized camp shop and pleasant restaurant — and the rather cramped nature of the adjoining beach — as you might deduce from a name like *Mikros Gialos!*
— **Camping Vasiliki Beach** (39kms direct, 45kms down the east coast). A large modern site on the beach to the west of the town. Shade depends on the rate at which the trees can be persuaded to grow under the rather windy conditions that prevail there. Open from April to Oct.

Levkas is better off for **water** than the other islands. Most of the traditional villages have springs which flow throughout the year; nor in Levkas town are you likely to miss the little fountain on your way to the main square.

Yachts can take on water (400drs per cubic metre) and fuel at quayside berths in Levkas town. A ship's chandler is close at hand, where gas bottles are easily changed. Hull and nechanical repairs can be undertaken;

Products

Levkas is fortunate to have fertile soil from which its hard-working and green-fingered population manages to extract a satisfactory harvest, despite some difficulties with the terrain. The traditional crops are olives, wheat and vines, as on other islands. Many of the olive trees are huge and twisted, though careful pruning maintains their yield. Vines are grown for winemaking, mostly red; whilst some local results are very agreeable, the bulk of it is best suited for blending. Citrus flourishes in the sheltered well-watered parts of the east coast, where vegetables are increasingly being planted.

A substantial amount of salt is produced from the salt-pans at Alikes, much of it traditionally used for preserving vegetables and fish. Whilst the latter is caught in the open sea from caiques, the town lagoon, which averages only a metre of depth, also contributes through fish-farming.

Much production goes on in the backstreets of the town, which includes furniture, barrel-making and metalwork, in addition to the yogurt and salami more obviously on display in the main street. The unique skills of embroidery and lace-making practised for centuries in some inland villages were recognised just in time to prevent them from dying out. Much of the credit belongs to the well-known collector Mrs Evangelia Gianoutatou, who was the first to bring a degree of organisation to the workers; choosing from among the best patterns and materials, she now sells these beautiful articles from her shop in the town and in Athens.

An island speciality is *savóro,* a mixture of various cold fried fish marinaded in oil and vinegar flavoured with currants, rosemary and garlic; it is more likely to feature on the menu of restaurants catering to local tastes. Another, less unusual, is *kokovetsi,* a form of grilled liver.

Cultural interest

The people of Levkas are deeply attached to their island, and their own part of it in particular; their healthy numbers and balance between the age groups has enabled the old customs to be passed on to the next generation. Traditional costume is still widely worn by older women, even in the town. This is based on a long-skirted full-flowing long-sleeved dress, woollen for everyday use, satin for best. Colours vary; black of course denotes the widow, whilst others wear various deep shades of brown, green, purple and blue. The throat is covered with a neck-scarf, except in the case of unmarried women. Many of the girls are strikingly attractive, whether or not attired in traditional dress.

The educated classes are equally engaged in promoting culture. Few other islands support free entrance to as many as four museums. And an extra special effort is made during two weeks towards the beginning of August, when an international festival of folklore has been held annually for the past 35 years. The first week is usually devoted to poetry, drama and singing, the second to dance. Performances take place in the central square — as at other times do concerts given by the town band.

Most villages have their local feast days. The most important begins on 11 August, when a two day event in Karia commemorates St Spiridon, and that day in 1716 when, not for the only time, he miraculously intervened to save Corfu (sic) — on this occasion from a Turkish siege. On (Orthodox) Whit Monday there is a morning service at the Faneromeni monastery, followed by feasting down in the town during the evening.

The offshore islands

Levkas administers a number of islands scattered off its east coast. The largest of them, Meganisi, has a frequent car-ferry service. Two other with substantial populations, Kalamos and Kastos, enjoy regular services by caique. Others can be visited by excursion caique, from Levkas town and Nidri. Although the more distant islands are well known among the yachting fraternity, few land-based tourists visit any of them — so the chance to pass twenty years back in time continues to exist.

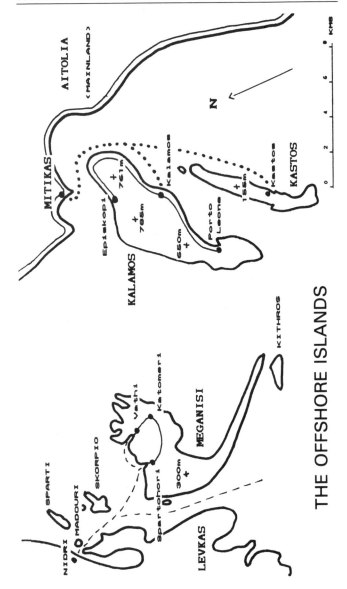

THE OFFSHORE ISLANDS

Meganisi

(Area 20 sq. kms, height 301m, population 1339)

The former caique service from Nidri has been replaced by a couple of open-deck car ferries — *C/F Levkas* based on Nidri, and *C/F Meganisi* based on Vathi, the chief port of Meganisi. In addition to the triangular service to Fiskardo and Frikes already discussed, these provide between three and nine daily services throughout the year to Vathi and Spartahori. From the latter's tiny jetty a 20-minute climb brings you to the small village perched on the edge of the cliffs. A good road connects it to Vathi via a third village, Katomeri. Rooms are available in all three. Weaving, spinning and wool-dying are cottage industries. The island is surprisingly green.

For yachtsmen Meganisi is a paradise because of the cluster of secure anchorages in the north east, and the variety of small deserted sandy coves they contain. There are also a number of interesting sea caves, but these can be visited only by boats.

The ferry from Nidri passes the small uninhabited islet of **Madouri**. This was owned for many years by the poet Aristotelis Valaoritis (1824-79), who devoted himself and his poems to the cause of Greek nationalism. He built the elegant Palladium-style mansion not only for his own use, but as a retreat for his fellow-spirits among the intelligensia.

The adjoining islands of **Skorpio** was acquired by the shipping magnate Aristotle Onassis, as home and mausoleum for himself and his dynasty. He himself lies buried here, as do his son Alexander and daughter Christina. The 1981 census shows a population of 7, all presumably family retainers. Whilst landing is forbidden, you can get a good view of the facilities during one of the caique excursions.

Kalamos

(Area 25 sq kms, height 785m, population 505)

The island is called after the reeds *(kalami)* which once grew plentifully here, and were harvested for screen-making. Though larger than Meganisi it has become depopulated; despite the remains of several windmills it does not even make its own bread any longer. The main supply port is Mitikas on the mainland opposite, to which a caique crosses from the island every morning. Should you want to go over at another time caiques from the island often fish sufficiently near to be hailed from Mitikas — enquire at the café near the central landing stage. The 'capital' on the south east coast,

The small town of Mitikas (left) faces the island of Kalamos (right). A newly-built coast road now makes this little-known part of Greece more accessible to the pioneering traveller.

also called Kalamos, sprawls raggedly down the hillside to the port, where fishing caiques are protected by a long mole. There is a good beach close by. A rough track connects it to another village on the north coast called Episcopi — the two communities are said not to get on well together! Accommodation can be had in the village rooms. There is a third deserted village at Kefali (Porto Leone). The soil is fertile, so olives and wine are produced, and animals graze. Caiques from Levkas town occasionally visit the island.

Kastos
(Area 6 sq kms, height 155m, population 68)
The small population of this little island all live around the tiny harbour in the south east. Conditions there are rather primitive, although electricity was recently brought in. Supply is from Mitikas as required — enquire at the café as for Kalamos above. Basic accommodation can be had in the village rooms.

Tailpiece I was sitting in a restaurant in Levkas town one evening, pleased with my day, I had called on a number of people, none by appointment; all of them had been so kind and helpful, pleased to give me as much of their time and experience as I could possibly wish. My mind went back to the old Greece I first remember, and its wonderful tradition of hospitality and friendship towards the stranger. At the next table a young German was paying his bill. "I come back next year," he said to the owner; "you have good people here, all is quiet, there are no problems." I think he was right!

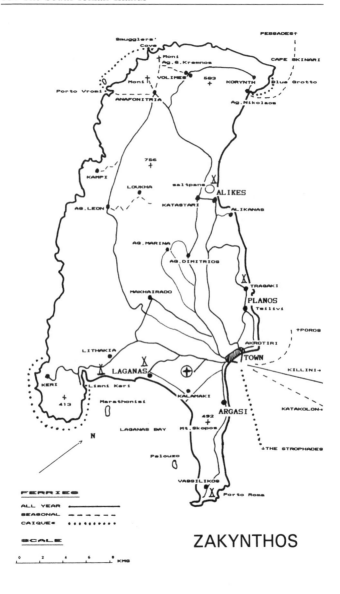

ZAKYNTHOS

THIRTEEN

Zakynthos

Population: 30,011   *Highest Point: 756m*
Area: 402 sq km   *Hotel beds: 4800*

Among their many island possessions, Zakynthos (Zakinthos) occupied a special place in the affection of the Venetians. *Zante, Zante, fior di Levante* they sang about it then, and flower of the Levant it remains even today, its central plain in springtime one vast garden of flower and blossom, colour and perfume. Combine that with another description of the island — a plain fringed by a horseshoe of hills — and you begin to appreciate the qualities that make Zakynthos different from other islands. The contrast is especially marked with its close neighbour, Kefallonia, the mass of whose own huge central mountain repels and disperses economic activity to the fringes of the island. The economy of Zakynthos, like the rainfall on which it used almost exclusively to depend, filters down from the hills, flowing through and nourished by the villages of the plain, before it concentrates within the mass of the capital — the island's single town and virtually its only port.

The sun continues to shine on Zante, which is consistently a quarter to half a degree Centigrade warmer than Kefallonia, and better sheltered. Such is the fertility of the land that fewer of its people needed to leave the island to find work. Nor did tourism, once it began to arrive in the 1960s, seriously compete with traditional activities for land-use and other resources. Fortunately, most beaches were bordered by marginal marshlands or hillsides not used for agriculture, whilst the drift of labour from agriculture to the tourist industry could be covered by higher productivity and a less intensive approach to cropping.

The people remain, as they were from the beginning, most friendly towards tourists, and virtually united in appreciation of the benefits that tourism brings to their island again, rather different from the more ambivalent attitude across the water. Whilst Zakynthos was a year behind in opening its international airport, on a comparison of charter flight numbers it now accounts for three times as much tourism as Kefallonia. Any internal arguments are confined to the distribution of benefits, and conservation of the island's natural assets. The recent moratorium imposed on further expansion at the four main existing resorts, in order to foster the development of new centres elsewhere in the island, accords well with the wishes of the majority.

Arrival by air

The airport is situated most conveniently on level marshland bordering the sea, only some four kilometres beyond the outskirts of the town. The terminal building is substantial and spacious, even with regard to the present high and rising number of flights using it. Domestic flights are met by Olympic Airways buses, international (charter) by their tour operators.

Summary of arrivals:
● Scheduled (domestic only):
— From Athens. 1 flight each day by Boeing 737. Duration 40mins.
— From Kefallonia and Corfu. Some of the flights from Athens to Zakynthos continue on to Kefallonia; similarly some Athens-Kefallonia flights, also by Boeing 737, continue to Zakynthos. Additionally there are a couple of inter-island flights each week from Corfu to Kefallonia and Zakynthos, by tiny Dornier 228 aircraft. Together these give an approximately daily connection to and from Kefallonia, besides a twice-weekly service to Corfu.
● International (charter only) flights from countries in north-west Europe — up to 65 flights weekly are projected for the summer of 1989, about half of them from the UK (airports include Gatwick, Birmingham, Bristol, Cardiff, East Midlands, Edinburgh, Glasgow, Luton and Manchester).

Arrival by sea

Arrangements are delightfully uncomplicated! More than 99 per cent of traffic from the mainland uses the port of **Killini,** travelling on one of four substantial conventional car ferries belonging to the consortium of ferry owners known as Kinopraxis Pleion *(C/F Dimitrios Miras,* 1500tons; *C/F Zakinthos,* 1200tons; *C/F Proteus,* 1000tons; *C/F Martha,* 900tons). The service runs continuously throughout the year, duration 1¼hrs, normal frequency 3-7 services daily, with extra unscheduled trips if traffic justifies them. All services go to Zakynthos town. The buses from Athens and Patras cross to the island on these ferries.

Between April and October it is also possible to embark for Zakynthos town from the mainland port of **Katakolon.** This is visited regularly three times each week by the *C/F Paxi,* primarily in connection with a tourist excursion its owner Zante Tours operates to Olympia; but passenger tickets, and also a dozen car spaces, are available to the general public. The ferry was initially bought for its seaworthiness on round-the-island trips, previously run by caique. Compared with a caique the *Paxi* is as a whale, but to most other car ferries it is little more than a sardine! However the venture has been successful enough to encourage plans for a larger replacement in 1989. Tickets for the *Paxi* are bought from the office of Zante Tours.

Tickets for Killini are sold from the Kinopraxis office between Zante Tours and the Strada Marina hotel. Advance reservation for vehicles is advisable, since demand for popular sailings often exceeds supply. When advance bookings close the police operate a

One of the frequent ferries from Killini entering the harbour of Zakynthos town, viewed from Bohali village on the Castle Hill. In the background the Argassi peninsula and Mount Skopos, scarred by the white slash from magnesium mining.

'priority late booking' system — just give your registration number to the officer controlling embarkation, and if he gives you the go-ahead, rush off and buy your tickets. Most of the ferries berth at the north breakwater, near an area half-way along it where the quayside has been built out. A small office here sells tickets whilst the ferry is actually loading. But one of the ferries seems to have inherited a divine right to berth directly onto the promenade, a practice which completely disrupts through traffic during loading and unloading, regardless of the best endeavours of the police team. The *Paxi* also berths in this area, but its tiny cargo causes no such problems.

Inter-island connections

Kefallonia is the only island with which there is a link, and that only in summer, when there are two or three possibilities:

— *C/F Paxi* runs across from Zakynthos town to **Poros** three times weekly — again in connection with an excursion.

— A new service recently started by the *C/F Mana Barbara*, an open deck car ferry that for the rest of the year plies across the Bay of Argostoli. This takes the shortest practicable route using two tiny and remote ports, **Skinari** in the north of Zakynthos and **Pessades** on the south coast of Kefallonia. The *Mana Barbara* spends the night in its home port of Lixouri, where embarkation and disembarkation are permitted. Motorists would be well advised to check on the current arrangements for buying tickets before leaving the appropriate island capital.

— In past years there have been a few summer sailings from Zakynthos town to **Argostoli** by *C/F Martha,* whose future is presently uncertain.

When none of the above is running, it is necessary to travel to Kefallonia via mainland Killini, which port is also used by the ferries to Poros and Argostoli (see Chapter 10).

Summary of ferries

● Zakynthos town-Poros. 2 or 3 x weekly April-Oct. 2hrs. *C/F Paxi.*

● Skinari-Pessades. 2 x daily July & Aug, 2 x 3 days a week June & Sept. 1hr +. *C/F Mana Barbara.*

● Zakynthos town-Argostoli. Chance of some summer sailings by *C/F Martha.*

Zakynthos town

Zante town was largely a creation of the seventeenth and eighteenth centuries; until then the people had lived on the hill above in the shelter of the Venetian castle. But as security improved, and the currant trade (see below) began to generate enormous wealth for all those involved, so the nobility and the new merchant class alike siezed the opportunity to rehouse themselves beside the harbour, in a manner appropriate to their exalted status, regardless of cost, and to the highest standards of prevailing good taste — which was naturally that of the occupying power. And so in due course Zakynthos inherited the finest testament to Venetian culture in the whole of Greece.

This legacy of dignified and graceful buildings, theatre and music, poetry and painting, which continued to flourish under British rule, and weathered the strains of reunion with Greece and the trauma of two world wars, came crashing down on 12 August 1953, in the worst earthquake to hit the island in four and a half centuries. Its consequences were practically as catastrophic as in Kefallonia, with only a handful of buildings undamaged, but the response was different. Whilst there were those who would have liked to develop a twentieth-century city from scratch, eventually it was agreed to attempt as faithful a reconstruction of the old part of the town as could be managed. It is now clear that the attempt has succeeded as well as might reasonably have been expected.

More than one third of the island population lives in this long narrow town, which extends some 3kms along the margin of the bay, under the shelter of the Castle hill. A fairly spacious promenade flanks the inner wall of the harbour, between the Church of Ag. Dionyssios at the start of the south breakwater and the large open space of **Solomos Square,** close to the north breakwater. This contains the expected mixture of bars, cafés, gift shops, and tourist agencies, whilst the **police station** is nicely situated in its centre. The tourist police officer is now housed in this building, where he can be as helpful as before, though he does keep strict office hours which don't usually include weekends. Nearer the square there are a couple of hotels including the large Strada Marina — which was the earlier name for the promenade, now called **Lombardou.** Adjoining the square is the **Town Hall.** Leaflets and some information can also be obtained from a small information

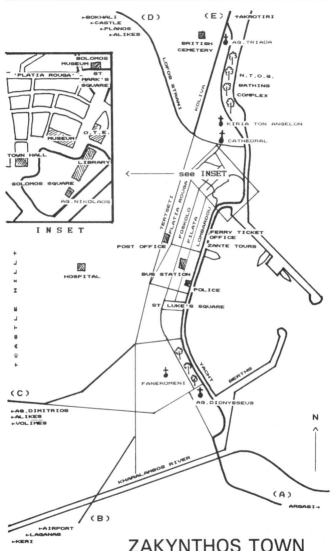

ZAKYNTHOS TOWN

office on its ground floor, manned by a couple of friendly English-speaking ladies (normally open 0900-1400 and 1700-2200, tel. 22713). To the left and beyond the Town Hall are clustered the town's three main banks.

Three blocks in from Solomos is the much smaller **St Mark's Square,** which nevertheless is the traditional focus of the town — the place where, for example, after Napoleon had occupied Venice in 1797, the people symbolically burnt the Golden Book and coats-of-arms of the hated 'puppet' nobility, and planted a tree of Freedom. Away from it and back parallel to the promenade runs the main street, much of it is now named **Alex. Roma,** but once called Platia Rouga (Broad Street). Most of the best shops can be found under its colonnades which, though concrete, give shade and some illusion of its earlier ambience. At the far end of the street is the **market** area for fresh foods; that and the nearby **bus station** give rise to several *souvlaki* stalls in this part of town. The more expensive restaurants are situated near St Mark's Square.

Several churches repay a visit if you find them open — the best times are Sunday morning and early any evening. The vast **Ag. Dionysseus** with its lofty white Venetian campanile beside can hardly be missed. It was the only church to survive the earthquake, which was fitting since it is named after the island's patron saint, whose remains and silver coffin stand in a gilded side-chapel; this together with richly painted ceilings and some huge ornamental chandeliers contributes to the sumptuous interior. The mummified body of Ag. Dionysseus is paraded through his town on 24 August and 17 December (see also Monastery of Anafonitria below). About 200m to the north west is the sandstone Church of the **Faneromeni** (manifestation); once the most splendid in the town, it lost most of its riches in the fire that followed the earthquake, but its fabric has been carefully reconstructed.

On the corner of Solomos nearest the breakwater is **Ag. Nikolaos sto Molo** (St Nicholas-on-the-Mole), a church dedicated to fishermen and the starting point for the town's elaborate Easter processions. First built as a chapel in 1483, it is the oldest surviving church, and one of the best restored. Further to the north, beyond the Xenia hotel, is the charming late-seventeenth century **Kiria ton Angelon** (Our Lady of the Angels), built for the guild of hairdressers, and also finely restored. Its key is kept at St Nicholas.

A few hundred metres further north, approached up a valley leading inland from the prominant Ag. Triada church (at the junction of Koliva with the coast road) can be found one of those half-forgotten British cemeteries (**Eglesika Nekrotafion**) guaranteed to delight any lover of the genre. Its gate is kept padlocked, the key in an adjoining house, but its easy enough to scramble in over a wall.

Back in town there are three museums. The **Zakynthos Museum** occupies an impressive building on Solomos Square, much of it taken up with housing a large collection of church art rescued after the earthquake, including the reconstruction of an entire small church. Several pictures of the town in former times should be of interest; some Mycenaean grave goods recently found at Kampi have already been restored and await display. Labels are in Greek and French. Open daily 0930-1430, closed Tuesday. Admission 100drs.

The **Solomos Museum** in St Mark's Square is dedicated to three of the great nineteenth-century Zantiote poets Dionyssos Solomos (1798-1857), Andreas Kalvos (1792-1869) and Ugo Foskolo (1788-1827) together with other native artists, musicians and even politicians. All the best-known works of Solomos were concerned with the revolutionary struggle. In addition to his 'Hymn to Liberty' — the first verses of which were set to music by Nikolaos Mantzaros to become the Greek national anthem — he wrote 'On the death of Lord Byron' amongst many other poems. His tomb and that of

Church of Ag. Dionysseus, one of the most conspicuous landmarks in Zakynthos town, seen from the promenade near the police station.

Kalvos, who lived much of his life abroad with his English wife and died in London, are in the museum. Foscolo, who wrote in Italian — the language of his father — is as honoured in Italy as in Greece. The collection contains some attractive locally-made furniture. Open 0930-1430, closed Wednesday. Free.

A newly opened **Museum of the Resistance,** devoted to the struggle during the second world war, is situated in the Library building on Solomos Square. The library itself is also of interest; in addition to its 20,000 books there is a permanent folklore display which includes historic photos, and part of the building can be adapted to serve as theatre, cinema or restaurant. Open 0700-1430, closed Saturday.

Culture can be topped off with a visit to the **Castle Hill.** This is approached by Lofos Strani, the main road slanting up the hillside, which can be joined beside the new Metropolitan church just to the north of St Mark's Square. Half-way up on the left is the Jewish cemetery, which bears witness to the substantial Jewish community on the island from the fourteenth century onwards. The small chapel on the left is Ag. Georgios, where revolutionary vows were taken by new members of Philiki Etairia, not only local boys like Solomos but also national leaders including the *klepht* Kolokotronis himself. Turn left at the cross-roads towards the top, and through the tiny village of Bokhali. The castle gate is opened from 0800-1800 daily except Tuesday, admission 200drs. It must be admitted that apart from the walls little remains in a condition to merit much individual attention, whilst several open cisterns constitute a positive danger to the unwary. But the walls, which offer superb views over the town to Mount Skopos (the sentry), enclose a large area of tall pine trees, delightful for an evening stroll. Several restaurants in Bokhali, including the prestigious Panorama, serve good meals — in the taverna Mona Lisa and the Quartetto di Zante (amongst others) sometimes to the accompaniment of live singing of Venetian style *kantádes*.

Getting about

Many roads, mostly tarmac, funnel out from the town to all parts of the island, as you can see from the town plan. In clockwise sequence, the promenade (A) extends over a narrow bridge across the Kharálambos river before running along the length of the Argasi peninsula. Possibly the best road on the island (B) leads south past the spur leading to the airport, and continues in reasonable condition as far as Keri. Also leaving from the south part of the town is the main road (C) through the central plain via Ag. Dimitrios and Katastari to Volimes and Skinari. An alternative road (D) to Ag. Dimitrios goes over the saddle of the Castle Hill; the Planos/Tsilivi resort can be reached from this road, or by another (E) running round the Akrotiri peninsula.

Few roads contrive to be straight, wide and well-surfaced at one and the same time, but this does add to the leisurely charm of the island, if also to the frustration of coach drivers trying to catch up on their slipping schedules. Pot-holes are sometimes abundant, whilst another cause of frustration for the tourist is an extraordinary lack of accuracy in all the **maps** sold on the island, which are particularly deceptive about the section between Tsilivi and Alikes, and also some parts of the south-west. There are plenty of **petrol stations** in and around the town, but they are still few and far between in outlying parts. Lithakia, Ag. Leon and Katastari are useful oases for fuel, but it is still wise to keep your tank topped up! **Buses** link Zakynthos town with all parts of the island, but are often intended to suit the convenience of villagers wanting to shop rather than tourists. Schedules vary according to season; but among the more frequent services are those to Laganas (up to 14 daily), Katastari (8), Lithakia (7), and Alikes (6) — most of the remainder are only two or three times daily, the first being very early in the morning. The Argasi peninsula is surprisingly neglected, so many people there rent their own transport.

Vehicle hire Many types of car, minibus, motor-bike, moped and bicycle can easily be hired, both from the town and the main resorts. Cars can be collected and returned at the airport. In 1988 the going rate for motorbikes was 1500-2000drs per day, mopeds 700-1000drs, depending on the period of hire.

Taxis There are about a hundred taxis on the island. The town alone has five taxi-ranks, and they can also be picked up at the main resorts and the more important villages. Fares are reasonable.

The resorts

The horshoe of hills enclosing the plain is interrupted not only at the mouth of the horseshoe (Laganas Bay), but also between the south end of Zakynthos town and Argasi, at Planos/Tsilivi, at Tragaki, and at Alikes. Each of these in due course became a nucleus for the development of tourism.

Church of Ag. Dionysseus, with yacht berths on the south mole in the foreground.

Argasi

This resort is situated only a couple of kilometres beyond the southern outskirts of the town; thus it was the first to be developed, and probably now includes the widest range of attractions to suit all tastes. Facilities spread up into the lower slopes of Mount Skopos (483m, ¾hr climb to the summit). Although the beach at Argasi itself is narrow and shingle, it has good facilities for windsurfing, paragliding and boat-hire, whilst there are a number of attractive sandy beaches further along the peninsula. It has plenty of restaurants, bars, discos, and night-spots, not counting many others in the town, where cinemas, tennis courts (NTOG organised), mini-golf and archery are also available.

Especially popular is the Captain's hotel, with fine views back to the town from its landscaped gardens and swimming pool. It is owned by Captain Christos Xenos, who runs it with a panache and involvement worthy of the president of the island hoteliers' association. Perhaps it is not surprising that the ladies should adore the gallant captain; but their male companions are equally devoted — no doubt his ability to drink any of them under the table, which he can sometimes be persuaded to demonstrate, has something to do with it?

Laganas

This has become a considerably larger complex than Argasi, although it started from little more than an empty expanse in the sheltered southern corner of Laganas Bay. The great attraction was and remains the enormous stretch of hard-packed sand that extends for 9kms between Laganas and Kalamaki, which is as ideal for sunbathing and watersports as for modelling sand-castles or racing motorbikes. Windsurfing, waterskiing, paragliding, boat hire and pedaloes are all to be had there, whilst Zante Diving offers sub-aqua facilities including instruction. The most popular part is fringed with rows of bars and tavernas, whose tables and sunshades spill onto the beach itself. A beautiful little rocky island just a stone's throw from the shore has been converted into a disco. The two more distant islands of Marathonisi and Pelouzo are ideal for under-water fishing, as well as nudism, which is acceptable there. The grid pattern of roads behind throbs with bright neon lights advertising everything needed to ensure a successful holiday devoted to sun, sand and sex! Here it is not at all difficult to forget that one is actually in Greece.

Kalamaki too has its own hotels, whilst the road between is already partitioned into building plots along most of its length!

In the hills above Laganas stand the stricken remains of Sarakina, until 1953 the finest Venetian *palazzo* on the island. It now belongs to the Mallias family, who have built a high quality restaurant on the opposite side of the road, surrounded by perfumed fruit-trees, shrubs and flowers. Under the discreet supervision of the founder and his wife the kitchens expertly prepare a wide variety of Greek dishes, whilst his multi-lingual son presides as Maître d' to give each guest a personal welcome. A meal with wine will probably cost a very reasonable 800-1000drs, which even includes free mini-bus transport to and from Laganas if required.

Planos/Tsilivi

Planos is the name of the village, whilst Tsilivi is strictly speaking the nearby beach — a whiter softer sand than Laganas, but there's still plenty of it. It is hard to realise that this village community of no more than 350 inhabitants can deploy 6 hotels with 250 beds, 500 rooms to rent, 12 restaurants and a pizza parlour, 10 cafés, one pub, 3 souvenir shops and 5 mini-markets. Nevertheless it remains the most informal of the resorts, because its buildings are diffused over a wide area, interspersed with orchards of olive and citrus trees and fields of grape vines.

English speakers should not hesitate to check in at the Olive Tree, not only to enjoy the pub itself, but also the company of its charming and well-informed hosts, Diana and Lakis.

The resort merges almost imperceptibly into the adjoining Tragaki, where the Caravel, arguably the island's best resort hotel, is already splendidly situated to overlook the sea — this area now looks ripe for the next phase of development.

Alikes

The village is named after its salt-pans which continue to produce, but its long sandy beach sheltered by the dunes behind it has proved irresistible to developers, despite being 'out in the sticks' some 19kms away from the town and airport. The resort is built on flat open land, so although much smaller its atmosphere more resembles Laganas than Argasi or Tsilivi. Windsurfing, canoes and pedaloes are available, and boat trips run direct to the Blue Grotto; there are plenty of places to eat and drink, and its first disco has recently arrived. Prices are generally reasonable.

Beaches

Almost all the better beaches have already been described. Not yet mentioned is the NTOG-organised beach and sports complex, situated on the northern outskirts of the town among lawns and shrubs. There are also remote beaches in the rugged west, which for practical purposes are accessible only by boat — from Limni Keri and Porto Vromi, for example.

A number of splendid sandy beaches towards the end of the Argasi peninsula require some special explanation. They are all self-evidently attractive to the passing tourist, whilst developers would dearly love to build hotels there. The problem is that they are also the ancestral breeding grounds of the loggerhead turtle *(caretta caretta)*, which has been using them for several thousand years at least — perhaps many millions, since it seems these turtles already existed at the time of the dinosaurs.

The adult loggerhead averages 1.2m length and weighs over 100kg. The female comes ashore only once every two or three years to lay her eggs, when during the long summer nights she will laboriously create three nests each containing about a hundred eggs. After 50 days the tiny turtles, about 6cms long, emerge during the cool of the night to make their way to the water. Already various natural predators are lying in wait for them; but should they be distracted by bright light — from hotels, discos or tourists bonfires — they will wander off in the wrong direction, only to scorch up in the heat of the following day.

The killing of adult turtles and the taking of their eggs were forbidden by presidential decree in 1980; the building of new hotels within 200m of certain sensitive beaches was more recently banned, and the loggerhead is on the EEC list of endangered species. Thus it is now the inadvertant activities of tourists which, directly or indirectly, represent the greatest threat. The driving of cars and motorbikes along the beach at night, and water-skiing offshore by day have already eliminated the turtle from Laganas, whilst even the planting of tamarisks for shade reduces the area of sand that gets hot enough to incubate the eggs.

Meanwhile a local community association is campaigning to have the area designated a national park. But perhaps tourists themselves, by their ability to influence tour operators and thus the authorities national and local, can also make a worth-while contribution to the cause of ecology and the loggerhead turtle?

The Akrotiri peninsula

This quiet, well-wooded area is easily accessible from the north of Zakynthos town, even on foot (¾hr). On the seaward side of the road, facing towards Killini, is the villa best known as the house of the poet Solomos (see Museum above) — though originally built as a summer residence for the British Lord High Commissioner from Corfu. Today it is privately owned. There is a choice of two circuits by which to return over the Castle Hill, the longer of which approaches the outskirts of Planos.

Keri

At 15kms from the town a ¾km spur off the main road leads along a reed-lined lakeside to reach the hamlet of Limni Keri, where small caiques wait at a pier to take tourists on local excursions to beaches, caves or off-shore islands. The shore of the lake has been notable for some pitch springs, which were even mentioned by the ancient historian Herodotus. No doubt today's flow is much reduced, though local fishermen are said still to collect it to caulk their boats. You are unlikely to be able to find one of the few remaining springs without help — the two oily pits near the pier are red herrings, being either wartime waste motor-oil tips or abandoned exploration wells, depending on which authority you prefer to believe. In any case there is little to be seen from the surface, for the traditional method of recovery is simply to push a rod down into a suitable part of the lake-bed, and withdraw it with pitch dripping from the end. If you want to try this for yourself, the solution is to mention your need to Augustinos, the extrovert host of the Kavouri taverna, who will summon a small boy to guide you to a suitable spot (small tip, naturally). On your return Augustinos will gladly serve you refreshment or a meal, should you wish it.

The village of Keri lies a further 4kms along the main road, which winds uphill through a veritable forest of olive trees. This unspoiled little village, which has a reputation for the quality of its bread, is centred on a small square containing a few cafés and tavernas. The church below the village is worth visiting, for its seventeenth century facade and a fine painted screen and icon. There are pleasant walks beyond, especially to the cliff-top where you can look down on the lighthouse, and one of those tantalising sandy beaches accessible only by boat. In April and August, here as in other parts such as the Argasi peninsula, hunters conceal themselves among the trees, as they lie in wait to shoot migrating pigeons.

Other excursions

There are a number of interesting **village churches** on the island, though you might need your own transport to visit them. Among the best are:

— **Makhairado** The church has an exceptionally fine interior, notable for its screen, and icon of Ag. Mavra. Its bells are said to be audible from every part of the island. The nearby unrestored church of Ipapandi has an attractive seventeenth century facade.

— **Ag. Marina** Some interesting architecture, and probably the finest screen on the island.

— **Volimes** See below.

The rugged cliffs in the north west can exercise a peculiar fascination. One of the best places to enjoy their drama is from beyond the village of **Kampi,** where a huge cross has been erected near the most convenient viewing-point. Even more rewarding might be a visit to the tiny harbour of **Porto Vromi;** this is being developed to open up the adjoining section of coast, since rough weather off Cape Skinari quite often prevents excursion caiques coming along the north coast from reaching it. The steep access road from Anafonitria is at present unsurfaced, but already small caiques run excursions, most notably to an otherwise inaccessible beach known as **Smuggler's Cove.** The story is a Zakynthiote 'Whisky Galore', in which a small ship full of contraband anchored, only to be driven onto the beach by a storm. It was impounded by the customs, but not before the local people, working with ropes from the top of the cliff, had helped themselves to most of the cargo. Shifting sands have now isolated the wreck in the middle of the beach.

An excursion to Porto Vromi is likely to be combined with a visit to the **Monastery of Anafonitria.** This was damaged in 1953 but restoration of its frescoes and carvings has been taking place recently. It contains a miraculous icon of the Virgin Mary, washed up from the wreckage of a galley which had escaped from Constantinople after its fall. Dionyssios (Denis) Sigouros was abbot here for 38 years; it is said that the murderer of his brother came here to beg him for sanctuary, which the holy man granted. He was born on Zante in 1547, worked and travelled on the mainland as a younger man, died on the island in 1622, and as Ag. Dionyssios became its patron saint. Both the island's major festivals are in his honour — on 17 December, when he died, and 24 August, when his body was brought back from the Strophades where at his own wish it had been buried. There is a café opposite the monastery. The less accessible monastery of Ag. Georgios Kremnos (St George of the precipice), where one lone monk has been living, lies equidistant on the rough direct track between the villages of Anafonitria and Volimes.

A considerable amount of road work has recently taken place in the extreme north of the island, of which the multi-level village of **Volimes** is the natural centre. Its seventeenth century church contains a number of art treasures, and there are schools for carpet weaving and cheese-making, both of which can be visited. A new road leads to Korynth and thence on to the lighthouse at the northern extremity of **Cape Skinari.** But the chief tourist attraction is a tiny port below Korynth, almost deserted but for an isolated hotel and a fleet of small caiques waiting to take parties out to visit the **Blue Grotto** and other caves. The Mediterranean has such grottos elsewhere which may well be even more spectacular. But this one hour excursion is a rewarding enough experience, especially if made early in the morning, when the white walls of the twin inter-connecting caves are bathed by the bluest of refracted light, and the massive bulk of Mt. Aenos glowers threateningly from across the calm transparent water. It is from this same mini-port, sometimes called Ag. Nikolaos, that the *C/F Mana Barbara* departs for Pessades in Kefallonia.

Accommodation

Hotels on Zakynthos

Class	Name	Rooms	Tel. (code 0695)
● In the town			
B	Kryoneri(Pension)	17	23567
B	Lina	46	28531
B	Strada Marina	112	22761
B	Xenia	39	22232

Class	Name	Rooms	Tel. (code 0695)
●	In the town (cont)		
B	Yria (Pension)	11	24682
C	Adriana	9	28149
C	Aegli	9	28317
C	Angelika	18	22391
C	Apollon	8	22838
C	Astoria	7	22419
C	Bitzaro	39	23644
C	Diana	48	28547
C	Gardelino (Apartments)	20	24333
C	Libro d'Oro	47	23785
C	Phoenix	35	22419
C	Plaza	18	28909
C	Reparo	15	23578
C	Tereza	30	24500
C	Zenith	7	22134
and 12 lower category hotels.			
●	At Akrotiri		
B	Akrotiri (Pension)	17	28000
●	At Bohali		
B	Varres	34	28352
●	In Alikes		
C	Asteria	18	83203
C	Astoria	31	83533
C	Galini (Pension)	8	83264
C	Ionian Star	22	83416
C	Montreal	31	83241
and one lower category hotels.			
●	At Alikanas		
B	Valaia	34	83223
C	Villa Santa Monika (Apartments)	19	83550
●	At Argassi		
A	Akti Zakantha	114	25375
B	Chryssi Akti	84	28679
B	Levante (Pension)	63	23608
B	Lokanda (Pension)	20	25563
B	Mimoza Beach (Bungalows)	44	22588
B	Yliessa	61	25346
C	Argassi Beach	33	28554
C	Captain's	37	22779

Class	Name	Rooms	Tel. (code 0695)
● At Argassi (cont)			
C	Castello (Apartments)	32	23520
C	Family Inn	16	25359

and one lower category hotel.

● At Kalamaki

Class	Name	Rooms	Tel. (code 0695)
B	Kalamaki Beach	29	22575
C	Crystal Beach	54	22917

● At Vassilikos

Class	Name	Rooms	Tel. (code 0695)
C	Aquarius (Bungalows)	16	25361
C	Vassilikon Beach	30	24114

and one lower category hotel.

● At Laganas

Class	Name	Rooms	Tel. (code 0695)
B	Esperia	35	51505
B	Galaxy	80	51171
B	Laganas	48	51793
B	Megas Alexandros	42	51580
B	Zante Beach (Bungalows)	252	51130
C	Alkyonis	19	51194
C	Asteria	12	51191
C	Atlantis	10	51142
C	Australia	17	51071
C	Blue Coast	10	22287
C	Eugenia	14	51149
C	Hellinis	9	51164
C	Ilios	8	51119
C	Ionis	50	51141
C	Margarita	30	51534
C	Medikas	10	51129
C	Olympia	17	51644
C	Panorama	13	51144
C	Selini	12	51154
C	Sirene	28	51188
C	Vezal	19	51155
C	Victoria	9	72265
C	Vyzantion	8	51136
C	Zefyros	11	72292

and 4 lower category hotels.

● At Planos

Class	Name	Rooms	Tel. (code 0695)
A	St Denis (Apartments)	8	25296
B	Dias	33	

Class	Name	Rooms	Tel. (code 0695)
●	At Planos (cont)		
C	Anetis	12	24590
C	Cosmopolite	14	28752
C	Orea Heleni	22	28788
C	Tsilivi	55	23109
●	At Tragaki		
A	Caravel	74	25261
●	At Korynth (Ag. Nikolaos)		
C	La Grotta	15	31224

Villas and rooms

A fair number of villas are available for rent, mostly in or near the main resorts. The police have more than two and a half thousand rooms on their books, though in fact there are probably more. In addition to the town and main resorts there are clusters of them in Akrotiri, Vassilikos and Keri — indeed few of the villages are without any.

Camping

There are three good campsites on the island, all quite recently built and well-signposted from the main roads.

Camping Laganas (Ag. Sostis) is situated amidst peaceful surroundings about 1km south west of Laganas. It is a medium-sized site, its broad level pitches well-shaded amongst massive olive trees, and with good services. Although part of the site is quite near to a sandy beach, in fact the distance from the gate is perhaps a little further than ideal; but there is a decent swimming pool on site, together with bar, restaurant and mini-market. It has recently come under new management. Open May to September

Camping Tartarouga is the biggest and highest category site on the island. Its situation is quite isolated, more than 3kms beyond Lithakia in the direction of Keri, and its 500m of access track might pose problems for a very large outfit. The well-wooded site slopes quite steeply down towards the private (pebble) beach, but the pitches are level thanks to a considerable amount of expensive terracing. Restaurant with bar, mini-market and beach bar. Open May to September.

Zante Camping at Tragaki is too recent yet to have been officially listed — though since it was ADAC recommended for 1987/88 there is little doubt that it soon will be. The reception, shop and restaurant are all close to the entrance beside the coast road, ½km beyond the Hotel Caravel. Pitches are widely dispersed on either side of a natural gulley which slopes down to a narrow sandy beach. Trees have been planted, but shade is still mostly artificial — though its position is better placed to intercept cooling breezes than the other more sheltered sites. Open May to September.

In addition there are several more informal campings, independent entities or operated in conjunction with a small hotel or taverna. Some can be found towards the end of the Argasi peninsula, and another, scruffy but very convenient for the beach, is located beyond the salt-pans at Alikes. No doubt they are cheaper than official sites, but you get fewer facilities for your money. Probably open between mid-June and mid-September.

Free camping is perfectly possible in outlying parts away from the town and main resorts. Water should be little problem, since most villages have a fountain.

Products

Agriculture flourishes on Zakynthos, the potential of its rich fertile soil impervious to competition from tourism. Many crops are grown, but **olives** and grape vines are predominant.

The beginning of the Venetian occupation, following a treaty with the Porte in 1484, found both the island and its population thoroughly run down following centuries of fighting. Venice had just previously lost its last possessions in the Peloponnese, which had been its main source of olive oil. Many former subjects there were brought over to Zakynthos, and successfully induced to make good the deficiency through a subsidy of 12 gold ducats per hundred olive trees planted. Today the best olive oil is amply good enough to justify finding space for it on the 'plane home.

At about the same time the **currant vine,** which had long been a minor crop of Corinth and other parts of the northern Peloponnese, was introduced by other refugees. Some 50 years later the first samples to arrive in England created a sensation almost comparable to that of tobacco and the potato. Quite rapidly currants became an indispensable part of the diet of the wealthier classes, who indiscriminately consumed vast quantities in bread, cakes, puddings, broths and stews. Before the end of the seventeenth century it required a British Consul and the supervision of half a dozen importing merchants to ensure the necessary tonnages. The British addiction continued to pour wealth into the island until well into the nineteenth century. Edward Lear, best known for his Nonsense Songs, visiting the islands only the year before the end of the British occupation, was able to write about 'this vast green plain ... one unbroken continuance of future currant dumplings and plum puddings'.

More conventionally vines are also grown for **wine-making.** Much of this is made into *verdéa,* a fresh dry green-tinged white of some potency. This is sold on the mainland and even exported; you can buy such bottles throughout the island, but it comes cheaper and often better direct from the cask.

Citrus fruit grows well in sheltered parts of the north coast, whilst **plums** prefer the lower inland slopes. **Water-melons** are a popular crop in some flat sandy parts, whilst so-called 'wild' **strawberries** from the hills, especially those of the Argasi peninsula, tempt tourists in early summer.

The colourful striped **carpets** of Volimes have already been mentioned, also that the village is the centre of the **cheese** industry. This is based on goat's milk, richly flavoured from the aromatic hillside grazings. Local people are well prepared to journey there, as Frenchmen make pilgrimages to their favourite *cave,* to make their personal selection from the past year's vintage of small hard round cheeses — which may well have lain a-pickling in barrels of olive oil during the previous twelve months. Another Volimes cheese is considered even superior to parmesan for grating.

Almonds, walnuts and other **nuts** are grown, and **honey** is collected from bees. Some of this is combined, together with sugar, egg white and vanilla, to emerge from several little 'factories' in the town as nougat, locally called *mandolato.* Other workshops produce **furniture** — you could even choose yourself a very economical fitted kitchen, if you had the means to take it home with you! More appropriate souvenirs for most of us would be some of the fine **perfumes** which are made locally by traditional methods. The leading producer is Razi, whose shop is on the Platia Rouga. For more than fifty years his family has arranged for wild flowers to be collected by hand and brought to their small factory on the outskirts of the town. Here they are macerated in alcohol and pressed, before the essences are distilled by freezing. Prices for these colognes are very reasonable in relation both to the generous bottle size and high quality of the contents. 'Clelia' and 'Fiorindo' are but two of Razi's more evocative fragrances.

A small amount of magnesite mining still continues from quarries on Mt. Skopos. Efforts have been made to tap the pitch reserves below Lake Keri; but there were no more successful than some exploratory drillings for oil, notably between Loukha and Ag. Leon, all of them insufficient for commercial exploitation.

Few of the earlier speciality dishes still survive on the menus of today's restaurants. One that should be found is a savoury beef stew called *saltsa*.

The Strophades

Zakynthos administers this remote group of islands, situated some 30 nautical miles to its south. The larger island contains the tree-capped ruins of a Byzantine fortress, built on the orders of the Empress Irene in 1241, which was subsequently converted into a couple of flourishing monasteries. In good weather it is certainly beautiful, and one can see why St Dennis chose it for his final resting place. One monastery is still occupied, however tenuously — for today's population according to the last census is only three, at least one of whom would be the lighthouse keeper. Were the islands nearer they would no doubt be a popular destination for tourist excursions. As it is they receive rare visits by a supplies caique from the town — and more frequent ones by transiting yachtsmen of discernment.

FOURTEEN

Excursions to the mainland

This chapter contains brief descriptions of some popular mainland destinations for tourist excursions from the South Ionian islands. Those in Central Greece are all easily accomplished by organised day trip from Levkas; those in the Pelonponnese can similarly be reached from Zakynthos. The possibilities of completing such a visit within the day from Kefallonia and Ithaka, or by public transport from Levkas and Zakynthos, are more uncertain, depending as they do on the precise timing of ferries and their connections.

Getting about

All the main roads involved are good or very good, and a number of buses travel along them between the major towns. Many of them start from Athens. Of these, the majority take the National Road on the south of the Gulf of Corinth towards Patras, which is a quicker route than the one along the north of the Gulf, despite the fact that you have to cross the Gulf on the Rion-Andirrion ferry (see below).

Buses between Patras and Thessaloniki may be convenient for some journeys, whilst in the north west of the Pelonponnese a fair number of buses run along the New National road between Patras and Pirgos — these towns are also linked by the quaint little Pelononnesos railway. (See also Chapter 4 under Rail and Bus travel.)

Rion and Andirrion

These two ports, at opposite sides of the entrance to the Gulf of Corinth, connect only with each other, by means of a very frequent ferry service which runs all day and night. Duration 15mins, frequency not less than every 15mins (every ½hr from 2300-0200 and 0500-0700, every hour between 0200 and 0500). More than 20 medium and large sized open deck car ferries are involved, and during peak periods several will be loading and unloading simultaneously. In addition to linking the two sides of the Gulf, the two embarkation areas form important interchange points for bus operations in the region. So if you want to go by bus to a town on the other side of the Gulf with which there is no direct connection, it is only necessary to take the ferry and wait on the other side. There is a direct bus service from Patras to Rion (11kms by the National Road) every 15mins, in addition to long distance services.

Andirrion, on the north side of the Gulf, has a couple of campsites in its immediate vicinity. Rion, on the south side, has at least three (Camping Rio Mare remains open all year). There are two more campsites on the Rion side of Patras (see Chapter 3).

Delphi

Delphi is one of the most important classical sites of ancient Greece and, despite the enormous number of visitors it receives, arguably still the grandest and most austerely beautiful. Its centre is a large Doric Temple to Apollo, within which a priestess known as the Pythia used to consult the Delphic Oracle. Political leaders began to come here in the hope of receiving backing for their intended actions; and with benefit of hindsight, such was the extraordinary success rate of the Oracle's predictions that in time Delphi became an important concourse for diplomacy, almost like some early prototype of the United Nations. It was also the venue for the Pythian Games, nearly as famous as the Olympic Games, with which it used to alternate every two years. The site is large, and set in hilly terrain under Mount Parnassos, so a full exploration is both lengthy and physically demanding. Outer clothing may also be advisable, for sometimes even in summer it can feel quite cool up there.

● Transport. The main road runs through the centre of the site. The modern village with bus station and tourist police is on a hill about 1km to the west.

● Camping. The Apollon at Delphi and Delphi Camping, 3kms to the south, are both open between April and October. Chrissa Camping, 6kms south, and Beach Camp on the coast are open all the year. Other campsites in the area.

Navpaktos

This charming little town, whose castle fortifications enclose a small harbour below it, is an admirable miniature example of the Venetian occupation, during which time it was called Lepanto. By 1571 it was temporarily in Turkish hands, and in active use as a base from which to raid the Ionian islands. On 7 October the fleet of Turkish galleys, together with those of their allies from Algiers and Tunis, sailed to meet a Catholic fleet led by Don John of Austria, bastard son of the Emperor Charles V. The ensuing Battle of Lepanto was fought near Missolonghi, and resulted in an annihilation from which Moslem seapower was never subsequently to recover.

> Don John pounding from the slaughter-painted poop
> Purpling all the ocean like a bloody pirate's sloop ...
> Vivat Hispania! Domino Gloria!
> Don John of Austria has set his people free!
> (G.K. Chesterton)

● Transport. The town is only 11kms east of Andirrion, with which it is connected by any of the buses travelling to the east.
● Camping. Camping Platanitis, on a beach between the town and Andirrion, is open from April to October.

Statue of Lord Byron in the Garden of Heroes, Missolonghi flanked by his native-born comrades of the Independence struggle.

Missolonghi

The town, though not unattractive, would be of little interest to tourists but for its association with the War of Independence and, especially for English speakers, as the place where Lord Byron died.

Byron's stay in Kefallonia, during which he strived unceasingly to raise funds for the patriots, and to induce some common strategy and purpose among their leaders, has been discussed in Chapter 10. On 4 January 1824 he sailed for Missolonghi to join Prince Mavrocordatos, who was defending against a larger force of Turks. He soon found himself in command of a regiment of 600 Suliotes, later augmented to 2,000 assorted mercenaries, for whose fighting efficiency, supplies and wages he accepted personal responsibility. After getting caught in a rainstorm whilst out riding, he developed a fever which his doctors insisted on treating with purgatives and bleeding by leeches. With the words 'The doctors have assassinated me!' on his lips, he expired on the evening of 19 April.

A Garden of Remembrance *(Heroon)* was established by King Otho, a short distance to the right inside the main entrance of the town. Byron's statue, with his heart buried under it, is in the centre, surrounded by memorials to the other principal heroes of the struggle. Admission free, but closed for several hours during the middle of the day — presumably to discourage vandalism.

● Transport. The town lies 41kms west of Andirrion, off the main road to Agrinion. There are a number of buses (westward) from Andirrion, as well as four daily direct from Patras, which call on their way to Agrinion.

● Camping. There is no campsite nearer than Andirrion, but free camping should be practicable outside the town — towards the coast at Tourlida, 5kms to the south, might be the best direction.

Nikopolis

Despite its Greek name this was a Roman city, built on a grandiose scale by Octavian (the Emperor Augustus), around the spot where he pitched his tent after his victory *(nike)* over the fleets of Anthony and Cleopatra at the Battle of Actium in 31BC. Nearly 100 years later St Paul was to write his epistle to Titus when over-wintering here. The remains include a theatre, stadium, basilicas, city walls and a museum — though for some reason most of its famous mosaics are now covered up. Open 0900-1500 daily except Tuesday, admission 200drs.

● Transport. The site lies some 8kms north of Preveza, on the main road to Parga and Igoumenitsa, to which there are several daily buses. Alternatively a taxi would not be expensive.

● Camping. Camping Monolithi, open April to October, and several others nearer Preveza.

Olympia

Olympia is, perhaps, the second most famous classical site in Greece, next to the Acropolis and Parthenon of Athens. Its name derives from Olympian Zeus, to whom it was dedicated in the remote past. Excavations show that it was already functioning in Mycenaean times — not as a city, but a sacred precinct. In due course games came to be held here in honour of Zeus, probably at first between local cities, but by 676BC on a panhellenic scale, every four years in July or August, at the time of the full moon following the summer solstice. For the period of the games an Olympic Truce was strictly observed, and individual athletes competed in foot, horse and chariot races, for a victor's crown of wild olive shoots and the honour of their native city. The games were suppressed by Theodosius I in 393AD, only to be revived in 1896 in a more modern form through the efforts of Baron de Coubertin.

The site is unusually verdant, its large area shaded by a multitude of evergreen oaks, pines, poplars and olive trees. Perhaps the remains outside, though numerous and substantial, are less impressive than might have been hoped; but the splendid museum, which contains several of the finest treasures of the ancient world — including pediments from the temple of Zeus, and a statue of Hermes by Praxiteles himself — does much to remedy any disappointment.

The large modern village is situated about ½km away, with a number of hotels, and many cafés, restaurants and tourist shops. Prices in many (but not all) of them tend to be expensive.

● Transport. Many excursions from Athens and the Peloponnese. An hourly bus service from Pirgos (¾hr, 120drs). The village is also on a branch line of the Peloponnesos railway, with 5 trains daily from Pirgos (½hr, 90drs).

● Camping. The three campsites at ancient Olympia include one, Camping Olympia, which remains open all the year.

Patras

The town was described in Chapter 3 (under The mainland: Where to head for) from the point of view of travellers in transit, but has sufficient to see and do for passing a pleasant day or two there. The Museum near Platia Olgas has a number of important exhibits, whilst the picture gallery in the Library building on D.Gounari is also worth a visit. In the open air the Platia Vas. Georgiou is encircled by pleasant neo-classical buildings linked by arcades. Higher up are the Kastro, on the site of the ancient acropolis above the town, and the nearby Roman Odeon, restored in 1960 since when it has been much used for drama and concert performances.

A pleasant excursion may be made to the Achaia Clauss wine factory, situated some 9kms to the south east of the town, which can be reached by No.7 bus from D.Gounari, just beyond the junction with Diakou. The firm was founded by the German Baron von Clauss, and has grown to become the largest of its kind in Greece. Its wines and spirits can be bought throughout the country, but most advantageously from the duty-free shops in the port of Patras. Tours between 0900-1300 and 1630-1830, free.

● Camping and Transport, see Chapter 3.

Castle of Chlemoutsi

This is the finest surviving 'crusader' castle in the Peloponnese, and among the best in Europe. It was built in 1220 by Geoffrey de Villehardouin, to control his new Frankish Principality of the Morea and its chief port Chiarenza, now Killini. There are superb views across to Zakynthos and Kefallonia.

● Transport. See Chapter 3 (under Killini in The Mainland: Where to head for) for the general situation. It is impossible to get all the way to the Castle by public transport, though buses between Neochorion and Killini Loutra pass the village of Kastro not far below (8 daily, 50drs). But a taxi from Killini would be much easier, and should not cost more than 1000drs.

● Camping. The three campsites in the Killini Loutra beach area include the NTOG's large Camping Killini, which remains open all the year.

Appendix A

The Greek language

The main reason for including this chapter is that the effort of learning a few words of the language will be repaid many times by the reception you will get from the Greek people. Just to wish an islander "good morning" in his language is like paying him a compliment and although he may then assume that you speak fluent Greek and proceed to rattle on at top speed, you will be instantly accepted and liable to some of the very generous Greek hospitality.

Some of the smaller islands have very few English-speaking inhabitants and so a few of the most commonly used expressions may be helpful but a phrase book is a worthwhile investment and this chapter does not aim to replace them.

All Greek words in this book are spelt phonetically and not in the accepted English equivalent spelling. The syllable stress is very important in Greek and to put it in the wrong place can change the meaning completely. The accent denotes the syllable to be stressed.

The alphabet

The Greek alphabet is confusing because some of the letters that look like ours have a totally different sound:

A α alpha	apple		Ξ ξ ksee	rocks
B β veta	never		O o omikron	on
Γ γ gamma	yellow or gap		Π π pee	paper
Δ δ thelta	then		P ρ roe	roe
E ε epsillon	enter		Σ σ sigma	sand
Z ζ zita	zip		T τ taff	tiff

H η ita	ch**ee**se		Y υ ipsilon	pol**i**ce
Θ θ thita	**th**ong		Φ φ fee	**f**end
I ι iota	p**i**ck		X χ hee	lo**ch**
K κ kappa	**k**ind		Ψ ψ psee	syna**pse**
Λ λ lamda	**l**ink		Ω ω omega	**o**n (or owe
M μ mee	**m**other			at the end
N ν nee	**n**ice			of words)

There are numerous letter combinations that make unpredictable sounds but this is rather off-putting for the beginner and so if you think you are ready for them, it is time to buy a teach yourself book.

Some conversational gambits

Meanwhile, it is useful to be able to form a few elementary questions and make one or two simple statements. Apart from ensuring your basic survival and comfort when there is no one around who speaks English this will, as said before, create a really friendly rapport with the local people.

The following lists will help you to put a few simple sentences together. Of course, these will not be in grammatically perfect Greek (a language cannot be learned so easily) but if you say them carefully they should be comprehensible to any Greek person, who will be absolutely delighted by the effort you have made. Remember to stress the accented syllables.

List A — basic statements and phrases

Yes: *neh*
No: *óhee*
Please/you are welcome: *parra kallóh*
Thank you: *efharistóe*
Good morning: *kallee máira*
Good evening: *kallee spáira*
Good night: *kallee níhta*
Hello/goodbye: *Yássoo* (*yássas* is more formal)
Greetings: *hyéretay*
Where is: *poo eénay*

I want: *thélloh*
I am: *éemay*
You are: *éesthay*
He/she is/there is/they are: *eenay*
We are: *ee már stay*
I have: *éhoe*
You have: *éhetay*
He/she/it has: *éhee*
We have: *éhoomay*
They have: *éhoon*
I don't want: *then thélloh*

Now if you turn to lists B, C and D you can add words to some of these to articulate your needs or ideas. Statements can be turned into questions by putting an intonation in your voice — to change "you are" to "are you?", for instance

List B — accommodation

hotel: *ksennoe doheé oh*
room: *thomátteeoh*
house: *spéetee*
bathroom: *bányoh*
shower: *dóos*

bed: *krevártee*
hot: *zéstee*
cold: *kréeoh*
blanket: *koo vérta*

List C — getting about

far: *makree áre*
near: *kondá*
bus: *leo for éeoh*
taxi: *taxí*
ferry boat: *férry bott*
street: *óh thos*
road: *dróh moss*
corner: *go neár*
left: *arist erráh*

right: *thex ee áh*
single: *applóh*
return: *epist rofée*
ticket: *ee sit ée ree ah*
post office: *tahee droh mée oh*
laundry: *plind éereeoh*
bank: *tráp ezza*
telephone: *telléfonoh*
petrol: *vrin zée nee*

List D — eating and drinking

restaurant: *eest ee at
  ór ee oh*
food: *figh eet óh*
coffee: *kaféh*
tea: *ts ígh*
breakfast: *proh ee nóh*
sugar: *záh harree*

salt: *a lár tee*
pepper: *pip áir ee*
wine: *krass ée*
beer: *béerah*
water: *nair óh*
without: *hórris*
oil: *lárthee*

List E — other useful phrases and words

As you gain a little confidence — and begin to understand the replies you get — you will probably be able to make use of the following phrases and words — when shopping, for instance. Note that, although days and numbers have been given here, it is more difficult to talk about time, such as the hours of boats and buses, so that is when you ask for it to be written down!

I want this: *thélloh aftóh*
I don't want this: *then thélloh aftóh*
What time does it leave?: *tee óra févyee*

What time does it arrive?: *tee óra ftáhnee*
Please write it down: *moo toh gráps etay parra kallóh*
Excuse me/sorry: *sig nóh mee*
I am an Englishman/woman: *éemay ángloss/angléeda*
Please speak slowly: *méelet ay argár parra kallóh*
Don't!: *mee!*
Go away!: *féev yet ay!*
Help!: *voh ée thee ah!*

Monday: *theftéra*
Tuesday: *tréetee*
Wednesday: *tetártee*
Thursday: *pémptee*
Friday: *parraskevée*
Saturday: *sávatoh*
Sunday: *kirree akée*

one: *énna*
two: *thé oh*
three: *trée ya*
four: *téssera*
five: *pénday*
six: *éxee*
seven: *eptá*
eight: *oktoé*
nine: *enay yáh*
ten: *théka*
eleven: *én theka*
twelve: *thó theka*
twenty: *ée cosee*
thirty: *tree ánda*
forty: *sarránda*

fifty: *penninda*
sixty: *ex índa*
seventy: *ev tho mínda*
eighty: *ovthónda*
ninety: *en en índa*
one hundred: *eka tón*
two hundred: *thee ak ówsee ah*
three hundred: *track ówsee ah*
four hundred: *tétrak owsee ah*
five hundred: *pént ak owsee ah*
seven hundred: *eptak ówsee ah*
eight hundred: *okt ak ówsee ah*
nine hundred: *enyak ówsee ah*
thousand: *hill eeyá*

Appendix B
Wind Force: the Beaufort Scale*

B'fort No.	Wind Descrip.	Effect on land	Effect on sea	Wind Speed knots	mph	kph	Wave height (m)+
0	Calm	Smoke rises vertically	Sea like a mirror	less than 1			-
1	Light air	Direction shown by smoke but not by wind vane	Ripples with the appearance of scales; no foam crests	1-3	1-3	1-2	-
2	Light breeze	Wind felt on face; leaves rustle; wind vanes move	Small wavelets; crests do not break	4-6	4-7	6-11	0.15-0.30
3	Gentle breeze	Leaves and twigs in motion wind extends light flag	Large wavelets; crests begin to break; scattered white horses	7-10	8-12	13-19	0.60-1.00
4	Moderate breeze	Small branches move; dust and loose paper raised	Small waves, becoming longer; fairly frequent white horses	11-16	13-18	21-29	1.00-1.50
5	Fresh breeze	Small trees in leaf begin to sway	Moderate waves; many white horses; chance of some spray	17-21	19-24	30-38	1.80-2.50
6	Strong breeze	Large branches in motion; telegraph wires whistle	Large waves begin to form; white crests extensive; some spray	22-27	25-31	40-50	3.00-4.00

7	Near gale	Whole trees in motion; difficult to walk against wind	Sea heaps up; white foam from breaking waves begins to be blown in streaks	28-33	32-38	51-61	4.00-6.00
8	Gale	Twigs break off trees; progress impeded	Moderately high waves; foam blown in well-marked streaks	34-40	39-46	63-74	5.50-7.50
9	Strong gale	Chimney pots and slates blown off	High waves; dense streaks of foam; wave crests begin to roll over; heavy spray	41-47	47-54	75-86	7.00-9.75
10	Storm	Trees uprooted; considerable structural damage	Very high waves, overhanging crests; dense white foam streaks; sea takes on white appearance; visibility affected	48-56	55-63	88-100	9.00-12.50
11	Violent storm	Widespread damage, seldom experienced in England	Exceptionally high waves; dense patches of foam; wave crests blown into froth; visibility affected	57-65	64-75	101-110	11.30-16.00
12	Hurricane	Winds of this force encountered only in Tropics	Air filled with foam & spray; visibility seriously affected	65 +	75 +	120 +	13.70 +

* Introduced in 1805 by Sir Francis Beaufort (1774-1857) hydrographer to the Navy
† First figure indicates average height of waves; second figure indicates maximum height.

Distance/Height

feet	ft or m	metres
3.281	1	0.305
6.562	2	0.610
9.843	3	0.914
13.123	4	1.219
16.404	5	1.524
19.685	6	8.829
22.966	7	2.134
26.247	8	2.438
29.528	9	2.743
32.808	10	3.048
65.617	20	8.096
82.081	25	7.620
164.05	50	15.25
328.1	100	30.5
3281.	1000	305.

Weight

pounds	kg or lb	kilograms
2.205	1	0.454
4.409	2	0.907
8.819	4	1.814
13.228	6	2.722
17.637	8	3.629
22.046	10	4.536
44.093	20	9.072
55.116	25	11.340
110.231	50	22.680
220.462	100	45.359

Distance

miles	**km or mls**	kilometres
0.621	1	1.609
1.243	2	3.219
1.864	3	4.828
2.486	4	6.437
3.107	5	8.047
3.728	6	9.656
4.350	7	11.265
4.971	8	12.875
5.592	9	14.484
6.214	10	16.093
12.428	20	32.186
15.534	25	40.234
31.069	50	80.467
62.13	100	160.93
621.3	1000	1609.3

Dress sizes

Size	bust/hip inches	bust/hip centimetres
8	30/32	76/81
10	32/34	81/86
12	34/36	86/91
14	36/38	91/97
16	38/40	97/102
18	40/42	102/107
20	42/44	107/112
22	44/46	112/117
24	46/48	117/122

Tyre pressure

lb per sq in	kg per sq cm
14	0.984
16	1.125
18	1.266
20	1.406
22	1.547
24	1.687
26	1.828
28	1.969
30	2.109
40	2.812

Temperature

centigrade	fahrenheit
0	32
5	41
10	50
20	68
30	86
40	104
50	122
60	140
70	158
80	176
90	194
100	212

Oven temperatures

Electric	Gas mark	Centigrade
225	¼	110
250	½	130
275	1	140
300	2	150
325	3	170
350	4	180
375	5	190
400	6	200
425	7	220
450	8	230

Your weight in kilos

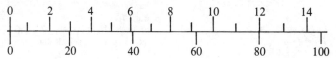

kilograms

Liquids

gallons	**gal or l**	litres
0.220	1	4.546
0.440	2	9.092
0.880	4	18.184
1.320	6	27.276
1.760	8	36.368
2.200	10	45.460
4.400	20	90.919
5.500	25	113.649
10.999	50	227.298
21.998	100	454.596

Some handy equivalents for self caterers

1 oz	25 g	1 fluid ounce	25 ml
4 oz	125 g	¼ pt. (1 gill)	142 ml
8 oz	250 g	½ pt.	284 ml
1 lb	500 g	¾ pt.	426 ml
2.2 lb	1 kilo	1 pt.	568 ml
		1¾ pints	1 litre

abbreviations: (Kef) Kefallonia; (Zak) Zakynthos